D1545479

JONATHAN SWIFT
AND
CONTEMPORARY CORK

JONATHAN SWIFT
AND
CONTEMPORARY CORK

BY GERALD Y. GOLDBERG

with line drawings by
SZYMON

and a foreword by
THE HON. CEARBHAILL O'DÁLAIGH
Chief Justice of Ireland

THE MERCIER PRESS

4 BRIDGE STREET CORK

PR 3726
G 615

92
S977go

Contents

TO:
Sheila, Nancy and Abigail
with love

Foreword

Already, before publication, at least one reader has found this a fascinating work. The author has taken Swift's associations with Cork as his subject, and in the compass of an essay he has succeeded in illumining the man, the period and the city. It must be for others more competent to say what place this work will have in the canon of Swift scholarship. This reader is content to note that Swift, in the tercentenary of his birth, has been worthily readmitted a freeman of the city of Cork and that no one in the whole of Munster could have made the honour more acceptable to the Dean than Gerald Goldberg has done. Handsome amends have been made by another lawyer for the machinations of Richard Bettesworth.

CEARBHAILL O'DÁLAIGH

9

Introduction and Acknowledgements

In the course of a lifetime spent with books I have become more and more conscious of the part which my native City and County of Cork has played in history, literature and the arts. With the exception of Dublin, no Irish City or County has been touched by events and personalities to the same extent as has Cork. From the time that St. Finbarr set up a seat of learning Cork has been a centre. Danes and Normans, Puritans, Quakers, Huguenots, English, Welsh and Scots have mingled their blood, ideals and cultures with that of the native Irish. Spenser found a home in County Cork, though not a haven and, there, he wrote the greater part of the last Cantos of the Faerie Queen. Sir Walter Raleigh left a name though not a reputation. The "Great" Earl steadily amassed estates from land formerly the property of the great Desmond Clan, which had conquered it from the native Irish. Cromwell, Marlborough and other English Generals battered at its gates, and Marlborough left a small Community of Marranos Jews, who formed the greater part of his Army's Commissariat, and whose existence was overlooked by Alexander the Coppersmith when he wrote his description of 18th Century Cork. William Penn became a Quaker in Cork City. John Wesley was stoned in its streets. The famous Cork accent owes much to its Huguenot citizens. The crafts of glass making and silverwork found their origins in the itinerant craftsmen who made their way to Cork from different parts of Europe. The famous Capt. Bligh of 'Mutiny on the Bounty' fame was one of its Freemen. The 'Fraserians' included four Cork men, William Maginn, Daniel MacClise, Crofton Croker and Fr. Prout (Mahony) whose contribution to 19th Century English Literature cannot be overlooked. Scott, Dickens, Thackery, Carlisle and other great writers found themselves within its walls. Swift too! He did not like the Cork Merchants and he tells us why. I have chosen the occasion of this, his Tercentenary to publish the first of a series of monographs in which I shall endeavour to bring together as much information as I can convey about Cork and Cork County. I have sought, in this slight work, to apply those standards necessary to a work of research and which require, as far as is possible, the use of original sources or, if not available, such tried and reliable secondary sources as have the hallmark of scholarship. I believe that I have brought together, for the first time, a concise statement of Swift's association by himself and his friends, with Cork. In particular, I have sought to unravel the reasons behind the objections made on the occasion of his being made a Freeman of the City of Cork. I have taken the feud between Swift and Bettesworth a little farther than has, ever, previously, been attempted; and, whilst there are obvious gaps in my 'proofs' I have, I hope, established a prima facie case in suggesting that Bettesworth had much to do with what happened. I have failed to find the missing Cork Freedom Box presented to Swift.

I cannot let the occasion pass without thanking the Hon. Cearbhaill O'Dálaigh, Chief Justice of Ireland for his kindness in writing so generous a foreword. My thanks are due, also, to Mr. Patrick Ahern and the staff of the Historical Library, University College Cork, where I was permitted to do much valuable study; to His Grace Dr. G. O. Simms, Archbishop of Dublin and the Librarian of the Representative Church Body for valuable information, to my friends Ashley Powell, Esq., Senior Counsel and Thomas A. Doyle, Esq., Senior Counsel for their valuable suggestions, comments and help, to Messrs John M. Tighe, Law Searchers, Dublin who unearthed at my request, the Memorial of property transactions between Sheridan and Swift and to all those who helped in various ways, some of whom are mentioned elsewhere. I wish to acknowledge, with sincere appreciation the permission which I have received from the Clarendon Press, Oxford to quote from the *Correspondence of Jonathan Swift*, ed. Sir Harold Williams, *Swift's Journal to Stella*, ed. Sir Harold Williams, *Swift's Poems*, ed. Sir Harold Williams, *Satires and Personal Writings*, ed. William Alfred Eddie; Messrs Basil Blackwell and Mott Ltd. Oxford, for permission to use Professor Herbert Davis's edition of the *Prose Works of Jonathan Swift*, The University of Illinois Press for permission to quote from Professor Oliver W. Ferguson's *Jonathan Swift in Ireland*, the Dolmen Press Ltd. for permission to quote from Sybil Le Brocquy's *Cadenus*, Messrs Hodges Figgis Ltd. who allowed me to use Dr. Denis Johnston's *In Search of Swift*, Messrs Methuen & Co. Ltd. for permission to quote from Professor Irwin Ehrenpreis's *Swift The Man, His Works And the Age*, Vol. I. I have made efforts, through Messrs Duckworth Ltd. to secure permission to use *The Orrery Papers*, ed. by Countess of Cork and Orrery, a permission, I am sure, which would have been readily granted and I take this opportunity of acknowledging the use which I made of this valuable work. I have used other works all of which are set out in the notes to the chapters of this Book and to the Authors and their Publishers I make due acknowledgment. I am conscious that much merit will attach to this Work from the excellent drawings made by my son, David Szymon, to whom l express my grateful appreciation. Finally, above and beyond all else, were it not for the inspiration and encouragement which I have received from the three ladies to whom I have dedicated this Work I might never have had the temerity to put pen to paper.

Cork – Hadley (New York)
April – Sept. 1966

Gerald Y. Goldberg

The Scene of Corke

The City of Cork does not sit 'solitary'[1] and even though, on occasions, she has wept 'sore in the night'[2] she is

'...great among the nations,
And princess among the provinces'.[3]

St. Finbarr, it was, who founded it – 'and he was then led by the Angel to where Cork is to-day, whence he settled down in the seat of his resurrection'.[4] Windele describes the City as occupying 'the centre of a deep valley of considerable extent, which stretches from east to west, and is enclosed on every side by a girdle of high hills through which the River Lee runs its course to the sea. This river, named in Irish the Luidh (the Luvius of Ptolemy) has its source in the mountain range which separates the counties of Cork and Kerry; issuing from Lake Gougane Barra, it flows along for about forty miles, when it divides itself into two unequal branches a mile above the City, which, after a separation of nearly two miles, again unite, and the river finally discharges itself into the Ocean to the South of Cove'.[5] The luckless poet Edmund Spenser, whom Queen Elizabeth created High Sheriff of Cork in 1598[6] and whose *Faerie Queen* was most probably conceived and partly written at Kilcolman Castle, Co. Cork, noted the converging arms of the river –

'Ne thence the Irishe rivers absent were;
Sith no lesse famous then the rest they bee,

. . . .

There also was the wide embayed Mayre;
The pleasaunt Bandon crownd with many a wood;
The spreading Lee, that like an island fayre,
Encloseth Corke with his divided flood'.[7]

And when the army of Hugh O'Neill drove back the English undertakers and they crowded into Cork, Spenser rode through that very same High Street described so vividly (as we shall note) by the Earl of Orrery in his letters to Swift, to take ship for London, where a month later he was to die, if we accept Ben Jonson's account, from starvation, in the gutter of a London street.[8] And Walter Raleigh, Spenser's 'Colin Clouts', whose estates adjoined those of his fellow poet, was to see service in the City already marked out as a 'haven royal',[9] a stronghold of the British crown, and was to set sail from Cork, on August 6th 1617 on his last voyage to the West Indies[10] – 'Haven royal' it might have been, but 'on the land side they are encumbered with evil neighbours, the Irish outlaws, that they are fain to watch their gates hourly to keep them out at service time, at meals from sun to sun, nor suffer any stranger to enter the City with his weapon, but the same to leave at a lodge appointed'.[11] Of the people of Cork Holinshed wrote – 'They walk out at seasons for recreation with power of men furnished. They trust not the country adjoining; but match in wedlock among themselves only, so that the whole City is well nigh linked one to the other in affinity'.[12] Cork received its first charter from John, son of Henry II, King of England, by which was granted to the citizens of Cork 'the same free laws and free customs as the Citizens of Bristol enjoy'.[13] The next Charter was granted by King Henry III dated Jan. 2nd, 1241-42 – 'the citizens not to plead without the walls but within their Guildhall... no strange merchant shall buy of a strangeman... but, only, of citizens... the citizens may marry themselves, their sons, daughters, and widows without license of the King...'.[14] This Charter was confirmed by Edward I, June 12th, 1291.[15] A new Charter was granted by Edward II, Jan. 20th, 1318.[16] Edward IV, Dec. 1st 1462 granted another new Charter and, at the same, time, granted Cork 'a custom called cocquet[17] for rebuilding their walls until they could travel a mile round their city in safety'.[18] King Henry VII, August 1st 1500, restored the Charter of the City, which had been disfranchised because of the part played by Cork in supporting the Pretender Perkin Warbeck.[19] A Mayor of Cork, John Walters, or Waters, members of whose family still survive in Cork City, was tried at Westminster, found guilty of high treason and hanged at Tyburn. He became the first Corkman, no doubt, to have his head set up on London Bridge. Cork's antipathy towards the reigning monarch is stressed by Warbeck in the declaration which he made before his execution –'... we there arrived in the town of Cork... they of the town because I was arrayed with some cloaths

Red Abbey, Cork

of silk of my said master. threaped upon me, that I should be the Duke of Clarence... and forasmuch as I denied it... After this, there came unto me an Englishman, whose name was Stephen Poytou, with one John Walter, and swore to me, that they knew well, that I was King Richard's bastard son... and then they advised me not to be afraid... and if I would do so, they would assist me with all their power, against the King of England...'.[20] King Henry VIII gave the City yet another Charter, with the right of the Mayor 'to have born before him within the city and liberties one decent sword sheathed, and that the sword bearer be adorned with a remarkable cap'.[21] Queen Elizabeth in 1576 confirmed all former Charters and in 1571 bestowed a silver collar of S.S. to Maurice Roche, Mayor of Cork, for his services against the Earl of Desmond.[22] Charles I granted 'the great Charter of the City',[23] and Oliver Cromwell granted another on 27th April 1656[24] 'which was only in force during his usurpation'.[25] After his death, Charles II confirmed all the privileges of the City on Jan. 16th 1662.[26] Queen Caroline, as regent, granted another Charter dated Jan. 1735 'which arrived at Cork Jan. 11th 1735 and cost the city £267'.[27]

One of the few acts of charity – indeed the only instance we know – with which Cromwell can be associated in Ireland, was concerned with his treatment of Edmund Spenser's grandson, William Spenser, who was deprived of his estates because he had become a Roman Catholic. He petitioned Cromwell, who wrote his Council in Ireland referring to the plea made by Spenser 'that being but seven years old at the beginning of the rebellion in Ireland... he repaired with his mother... to the City of Cork... that he never bore arms against the Commonwealth of England, that his grandfather Edmund Spenser, and his father, were both Protestants, from whom an estate of land in the barony of Fermoy in the County of Cork, descended upon him... that the said estate hath been lately given to the soldiers in satisfaction of their arrears, only upon the account of his professing the Popish religion which, since his coming to years of discretion he hath, as he professes, utterly renounced. That his grandfather was... Spenser... and if, upon inquiry, you shall find his case to be such, we judge it just and reasonable... that he be forthwith restored to his estate...'.[28]

The purpose of the foregoing remarks is not so much to provide a short epitome of the history of Cork, as to prepare our readers for the remarkable observations made by John, fifth Earl of Orrery, and fifth Earl of Cork, of the City and its people. Orrery was a descendant of Richard Boyle, first Earl of Cork contemporary in County Cork with Edmund Spenser and Sir

Walter Raleigh. Richard Boyle's public career and deeds encompass the most important and significant years of the Elizabethan age in Munster.[29] Those who would wish to see a remarkable Elizabethan monument would do well to visit Youghal, Co. Cork, where he lies surrounded by the effigies of his two wives and fifteen children. His son, Lord Broghill 'concentrated together and formed into a Borough, the villages of Rathgogan and a smaller adjacent one, which he named the town of Charleville'[30] Co. Cork: Orrery belonged 'rather to the class of Litterateurs than of Authors, being diligent and studious, and what in those days were termed 'elegant scholars'.[31] His first tutor was 'Mr. Fenton – the collaborator of Pope in the Odyssey'.[32] His family business brought him from time to time to Cork where he formed a close association with Dr. Edward Barry M.D., Fellow of the Royal Society, and his Majesty's Physician General to the army in Ireland, and who was then living in Cork. Of Barry, Orrery could write to Alexander Pope:

'And now let me make you acquainted with the Gentleman in whose House I live, and who honours me with his friendship. He is a man in whose breast all the Virtues centre: of great Learning, and a sweetness of Temper scarce to be parallel'd. His Study has been physick; and tho' a young man he is at the head of his profession. Buried at Corke, his uncommon fine qualities move in too narrow a sphere: nor will so valuable a jewel shine in its full Lustre till he goes to Dublin'.

In his correspondence with Swift and Barry, Orrery provides an illuminating picture of life in Cork. At the same time, Orrery was closely associated with Swift, and whilst it appeared that Orrery held Swift in the highest regard and veneration, he took occasion, when Swift was dead, to publish *Remarks on the Life and Writings of Dr. Jonathan Swift*[33] which, from various points of view, have been severely criticised. Thus, whilst he acknowledged Swift's friendship 'was an honour to me'[34] he was vain enough to claim 'I have even drawn advantage from his errors'.[35] He had beheld Swift, he said, 'in all humours and dispositions... his capacity and strength of mind were undoubtedly equal to any talk whatever. His pride, his spirit, his ambition, call it by what name you please, was boundless... he was sour and severe, but not absolutely ill-natured. He was sociable only to particular friends, and to them only at particular hours. He knew politeness more than he practised it. He was a mixture of avarice and

18

generosity; the former was frequently prevalent; the latter seldom appeared unless excited by compassion. He was open to adulation, and could not, or would not, distinguish between low flattery, and just applause. His ambition rendered him superiour to envy. He was undisguised and perfectly sincere... His perpetual views were directed towards power'.[36] Later he says – 'His spirit, for I would give it the softest name, was ever untractable. The motions of his genius were often irregular. He assumed more the air of a patron than of a friend – he affected rather to dictate than advise. He was elated with the appearance of enjoying ministerial confidence. He enjoyed the shadow, the substance was detained from him. He was employed, not trusted; and at the same time that he imagined himself a subtil diver, who dextrously shot down into the profoundest regions of politics, he was suffered only to found the shallows nearest the shore, and was scarce admitted to descend below the froth at the top. Perhaps the deeper bottoms were too muddy for his inspection'.[37] It is no part of this work to offer comment on the justness or otherwise of these views. With one opinion, later expressed, we are in agreement – 'Swift takes pleasure in giving pain'.[38] Orrery had come to Cork for the purpose of investigating his estates and of putting them in order.[39] He implores the Earl of Stafford – '...to remember an humble servant buried in Ireland. Parchments and potatoes have for some time put all thoughts of England out of my head'.[40] He provides a wonderful picture of a social event in Cork[41] – 'O Sacred Silence, How I adore Thee! I have passed this day amidst the Confusion of Babel! I have been at a Feast. Paper Mills, Thunder, and the King's Kitchen are soft Music to the noises I have heard. Nonsense and Wine have flowed in plenty, gigantic Saddles of Mutton and Brobdingnaggian Rumps of Beef weigh down the Table. Bumpers of Claret and Bowls of White-Wine were perpetually under my nose... This short sketch may give you some faint idea of our Entertainments in this part of the world... these are esteemed according to the Quantity, not to the Quality of the Victuals...' Of his Host he writes – '... He is stupidly gay. The commencement of his gaiety bubbles up in coarse Laughs, which gradually increase after every Brimmer, till they join Chorus with Oaths, Curses and Blasphemies, Filth, Obscenity and Rudeness of every sort is the wit of the day and He that can be most beastly, most impudent and most absurd, carries off the Laurel of the Triumph'.[42] His opinion of Corkmen is less than favourable, for he protests that he never stays long 'at the Hibernian Games, but hastening home as fast as possible cannot help wondering what Mansions in the

Elysian Fields are allotted to those Heroes whose Delight consists in variety of Folly, Distraction and Drunkenness'.[43]

But soon the Earl of Orrery has to write a letter to Jonathan Swift, Dean of St. Patricks. It is an important letter, one which we feel he was asked to write. It was not easy to write it. We suspect that he did not want to write it. Its connection with the unhappy circumstances surrounding Swift's honorary Freedom of Cork suggests that Orrery was, only, a pawn in the efforts which were made to soften the heavy blow which Swift's enemies dealt him.[44] For us it is an historic and important letter, which will be the subject of further comment. For Orrery it was to bring a typical Swiftian rebuff – 'I am sorry there are not fools enough in Cork to keep you out of the Spleen'. The letter is cautious in its approach towards its main object, seeking first to put the Dean in good humour and to please him with a description of Cork and its people which, perhaps, the Dean might be glad to receive. Thus – 'The Scene of Corke is ever the same: dull, insipid, and void of all Amusement: His sacred Majesty was not under greater difficulty to find out Diversions at Helvoetsluys, than I am here: The Butchers are as greasy, The Quakers as formal, and the Presbyterians as holy and full of the Lord as usual: All Things are in the statu quo: even the Hogs and Piggs gruntle in the same cadence as of yore. Unfurnish'd with variety, and drooping under the natural dullness of the Place, materials for a Letter are as hard to be found, as Money, Sense, Honesty, or Truth'.[45] Orrery's aversion to Cork is expressed in other letters, which he wrote to his friend Tom Southerne. Thus, on March 10th 1732-3 he described the City as 'this Melancholy place... I stand in need of very strong Restoratives to preserve the Gloom and Horror of this City from enveloping my Heart'.[46] Five days after his letter to Dean Swift, Orrery was to open a letter to Southerne with this descriptive note of Cork – 'My Dear old man, I have quitted Dublin and its alluring pleasures for the ox-slaying City of Cork'.[47] He may have known Swift's feelings about Cork and its citizens, for some four years earlier, Swift was to write Dean Brandreth – 'Cork indeed was a place of trade; but for some years past has gone into decay and the wretched merchants instead of being dealers, are dwindled to pedlars and cheats'.[48] If this were ever to become known to the merchants of Cork, it would cost him dear. Therefore he appeals to Brandreth – 'I desire you will not write such accounts to your friends in England'.[49] Yet, if Dean Swift did not like Cork, it was not as a City that he thundered against it; but against those who, as elsewhere in the country, were the ruling class –'I never yet saw in Ireland a spot of earth two feet wide, that had not in it something to displease'.[50] He was equally censorious of Tipperary – 'I think I was once in your county, Tipperary, which is like the rest of the Kingdom, a bare face of nature, without houses or plantations; filthy cabins, miserable, tattered, half-starved creatures, scarce in human shape... every male and female, from the farmer inclusive to the day-labourer, infallibly a thief, and consequently a beggar, which in this island are terms convertible'.[51] He makes it clear that 'all these evils are effects of English tyranny; so your sons and grandchildren will find to their sorrow',[52] and it was in this context that he made his remarks about Cork. It must also be remembered, as Prof. Oliver W. Ferguson says, that – 'as a Protestant Anglo-Irishman, Swift was a member of a privileged class',[53] and that following upon the outbreak of the Revolution of 1689 in Ireland, the supremacy of the Anglo-Irish had been seriously jeopardised. Ireland, as G.M. Trevelyan points out 'was the Achilles' heel of the Revolution Settlement'.[54] The arrangements made after the re-conquest by William 'lasted for ninety years unchanged. But they rested on force alone'.[55] Whilst 'the thoughts of the English were diverted to agricultural and industrial change and enterprise at home, Ireland, meanwhile, moodily ate her potatoes at the door of her hovel and brooded in her savage poetic heart over ancient wrongs still unremedied, and griefs ever fresh from year to year'.[56] In the City of Cork, therefore, in 1732 whilst there were, according to a return made by the hearth-money collectors 2,569 Protestant and 5,398 Roman Catholic families[57] control of the City was firmly vested in Protestant hands, and the situation of Roman Catholics was not a happy one. Thus, in 1702 an attempt was made by the Corporation of Cork to reduce the petty duties payable by a Protestant trader to her majesty's Custom 'it being wrong to the Commons to permit Papists to enjoy such a privilege, and would be an encouragement for others to flock into this City, to the impoverishment of the Protestants by taking away their trade'.[58] Again, in 1706, the Corporation of Cork, on the complaint of the Master, Wardens and Company of Coopers, ordered that the persons therein complained of be served with an order 'not to follow their trades within the City, suburbs or liberties'.[59] These included 'Irish Papists who have no right to their freedom, have lately come and set up, and drive the coopering trade within the City, suburbs, and liberties, and take as many apprentices as they do please, and employ as many journeymen as their occasions require, who, being generally Papists, flock to them, which, if not prevented, will tend to the impoverishing several of the Protestant Coopers, and the unskilfulness of several of these new comers will bring disreputation upon the Cooperage of this City'.[60] The pressure exerted against Catholics at the time is still further exemplified by the resolution of the Corporation passed on 17th May 1709 in the following terms:

'Whereas it is conceived necessary this present session of Parliament for the preservation of the Protestant interest and support of the trade of the cities and towns in the Protestant hands by endeavouring to debar the Papists from carrying on any foreign trade, which they are running into and which they will in all likelyhood (if not seasonably prevented) ingross to themselves, to the unspeakable prejudice of the Protestant merchants and traders, and hinderance of foreign Protestants from coming over with their stocks, that Agents should be sent out of their respective cities and towns to Dublin to solicit Parliament for redress'.[61]

Swift summed up this anti-Catholic attitude in a letter which he wrote to Alexander Pope on May 2nd 1730 in these words: '…we have no other zeal or merit than what arises from the utter detestation of your Religion'.[62] But, to return to Orrery's letter, which deftly highlights some of the features of life in Cork City – the nature of trade, the different religious groups. Swift knew of the Quakers, and had some remote interest in their experiences in Cork. He knew and liked William Penn, whose father had considerable estates in County Cork, where Penn spent several years, as a boy, in their Castle at Macroom. 'Mr. Harley came out to me… and presented me… among others, Will Penn, the Quaker'.[63] A year later, on Jan 12th 1711-12 he records – 'I was very deep with the duke of Ormond to-day at the Cockpit, where we met to be private… My friend Penn came there, Will Penn the Quaker, at the head of his brethren, to thank the duke for his kindness to their people in Ireland'.[64] He finds something about their appearance amusing – 'to see a dozen scoundrels with their hats on, and the duke complimenting with his off was a good sight enough'.[65] Penn became a Quaker in the City of Cork in 1667 as a result of words spoken by one Thomas Loe to a text 'There is a faith which overcomes the world and there is a faith which is overcome by the world',[66] and his adherence to his beliefs resulted in imprisonment, in Cork, on several occasions. Because of his friendship with leading men in the government, Penn was of great use in stemming the persecution of Friends.[67] 'Friends in Ireland were almost of English birth... as in England their known honesty made them successful in business and as Penn himself suggests, part of the hostility towards them was from this very cause... in the towns there were jealousies and petty-mindedness, which supported by the attitude of the clergy, caused Quakers much suffering. They were distrained for tithe...'[68] So it was that Penn with his family connections was able to call on men like Orrery and Ormond for help, and to win the respect of men like Swift. In the City of Cork the pressures were heavy upon them – 'That Jon. Hammon and other Quakers pay their tolleration money as usual, or in default they lose the benefit of the tolleration, and pay petty duties and gatcage'[69] was one of the orders made by the Cork Corporation on Nov. 10th 1690; but, when money was needed, the same Corporation did not hesitate to resolve – 'Whereas there are several poor Protestants in this town not able to advance money for dieting the soldiers quartered on them. Ordered that application be made to the Quakers, and other monied men of this town, by way of loan, until the King's pay shall come to the army, that they would advance a considerable sum?'[70] Life was made very unpleasant for them, so much so that on more than one occasion Penn appealed, on behalf of his afflicted brethren, to the then Lord Orrery who, in his reply of May 16th 1607, said – '...I much wonder how the Major of Corke should give any Gentleman bee hee of what Religion or sect soe ever such ill language as you send me word he gave you, for severall sorts of Religion is but variety of opinions, which certainly cannot make any man degenerate from being a gentleman who was born soe, and although the Major of Corke and you differ about Religion yet he ought to show you that Civility as your birth requires; I shall come very speedily to Corke and then I'le gitt him to deliver you yre books.'[71]

Orrery differentiates between the formality of the Quakers, which Swift notes, and the Presbyterians 'as holy and full of the Lord as usual.[72] Swift, as an Anglican churchman, considered them an evil –'... you know the Dissenters in Ireland are suffered to have their conventicles only by connivance, and that only in places where they formerly used to meet... It has been the weakness of the Dissenters to be too sanguine and assuming upon events in the State which appeared to give them the least encouragement; and this, in other turns of affairs, hath proved very much to their disadvantage. The most moderate Churchmen may be apt to resent when they see a sect, without toleration by law, insulting the average Religion...

I hope, therefore, you will not think it hard if I take those methods which my duty obliges me, to prevent this growing evil, as far as it lies in my power'[73] he wrote to Sir Arthur Langford on Oct. 30th, 1714. G. M. Trevelyan says – 'The light of the Presbyterians in Ireland was not hid under a bushel. When their synods were called together, they would sometimes enter the town in a public cavalcade, every minister being attended by a layman on each hand, well armed to the great terror of such of her Majesty's subjects as are of the Church of Ireland'.[74] The accuracy of Orrery's observations is, at once, observed from the complaint of the Presbyterian community of Cork to the Corporation of Cork on 23rd July 1706:

'Upon complaint by Samuel Lowther, Preacher of God's Word on behalf of himself and the congregation of dissenting Protestants, called Presbyterians, within this City under his charge, setting forth that the neighbourhood of the meeting-house by them set apart for the worship of God, in the land called Watergate Lane, do very much annoy their congregation by making dunghills in the said lane, especially upon a vacant place belonging to this Corporation, being anciently a market-place, near the said meeting-house, the stink whereof is many times offensive, and therefore for prevention thereof for the future, prayed such a grant from this board as may enable them at their own charge to put the said street and vacant place adjoining to their said meeting-house in good repair, and to keep the street clean and decent as it ought to be, prohibiting all and all manner of persons whatsoever from putting any dung or dirt thereon'.[75]

The decision of the Corporation is an example of tolerance unusual on those days, because:

'This board not being willing any annoyance or inconveniency should be put upon any persons in the service of God Almighty, but that all places set apart for his worship should be kept sweet and decent, ordered, that all such persons who have any dung or rubbish on the premises do forthwith remove same, and for the future no person do presume to lay any dirt in said vacant place or the street adjoining said meeting-house, which may incommode the congregation, on pain of being punished as severely as the law will allow and that said vacant place and street, during the pleasure of the Mayor, etc, be put under the care of said Samuel

Lowther, and his successors and congregation, to be kept a clean open street adjoining to their Meeting-house'.[76]

The degree of tolerance which this Order exhibited can be understood, only, when considered in relation to the divisions between the members of the established Church and the Protestant dissenters. Although the Presbyterians, the most important group of dissenters, were strongly established 'they were not legally granted the same status with dissenters in England until the Toleration Act of 1719; and the Sacramental Test Act (passed in 1704 and not repealed until 1780) excluded them from civil and military posts'.[77] The same degree of tolerance was not forthcoming in relation to the Catholic people of Cork. Ferguson explains that 'In the oppression of the Catholics, the members of the established Church and the Protestant dissenters were in full agreement, but in all else they were divided'.[78] Thus the Presbyterians, although naturally opposed to the Test clause, 'they were willing to submit to it in order more thoroughly to suppress the Catholics'.[79]

Whatever the accuracy of his observations regarding the religions, manners and customs of Cork, and of which we shall hear more, Orrery could not have been sincere when he described the scene as 'dull, insipid and devoid of all amusements'. For example, William Smith Clark notes that 'early in the Spring (1713) the directors' (of the Smock Alley Players in Dublin) 'had taken steps to extend stage activities to Cork'[80] which Clark describes as 'the fastest growing City in Ireland. An ambitious but still ugly metropolis of twenty-five to thirty thousand inhabitants... thriving beyond all other Irish ports on account of its immense export of provisions (such as pork, butter, tallow, hides, wool, and yarn) to the American colonies, the West Indies, Spain, and France...[81] When Orrery tells Swift 'I have not yett been upon the Change' he is referring to the Exchange, which was opened on or about May 1st 1710 'the bell to be tolled at eleven o'clock every day and continued half an hour'[82] and which Smith pronounced as being 'in excellent proportion... the neatest and most regular of the kind in Ireland'.[83] The second story of the Exchange contained assembly rooms, the gathering place of 'the quality'. Rich merchants, many of them either English Quakers, or French Huguenot emigres, formed the backbone of Cork Society, a Society which, as a result of its mercantile contacts, had tended to develop Continental manners of elegance and cultivation. And MacLysaght noted that 'The people follow pretty much the French air in conversation, bringing up their children to dance, play on the fiddle, and fence, if they can give them nothing else'.[84] Smith adds – 'In this City is a good theatre, where the Comedians from Dublin entertain the town generally during the Summer assizes, and a month or two longer as they meet with encouragement. There is also a smaller one in Broad Lane... here are... two coffee houses, both near the exchange, they are much frequented, and besides the English news-papers, have most of the Dublin ones: The better sort are fond of news and politics and are well versed in public affairs'.[85] That Cork was not entirely an 'ox-slaying city' is more than evidenced by Sir Charles J. Jackson's notes – 'In the seventeenth and eighteenth centuries very large quantities of plate were manufactured in Cork and the business of Goldsmith was so remunerative that many leading County families in the South of Ireland were pleased to apprentice their sons to members of the Craft in Cork... The situation of Cork with its natural harbour... and its proximity to the Spanish peninsula and the west of France afforded unparallelled advantages for intercourse with those countries whence the City received not only supplies of silver but immigrant craftsmen'[86] who brought with them their knowledge of designing as practised by the goldsmiths of the continent of Europe. The theatre in Cork in mid-July 1733, 1735, and 1736 appears to have been strongly established, but is passed over by Orrery. One notes, also, the number of 'entertainments' and 'celebrations' which the Corporation of Cork were quick to hold, upon every reasonable opportunity.

But theatre and 'Hoggs and Piggs' and greasy butchers and goldsmiths and merchants and sailors and soldiers must, perforce, continue to live together – 'one year with another there were near a hundred thousand bullocks and cows slaughtered in this City, from August to Christmas' and 'for packing, salting and barreling beef, this City gives place to no other in Europe... salt beef imported into the towns of Havre, Nants, St. Maloes, Rochell, Bordeaux and Brest, in order to be exported again to the French American colonies'.[87] Rev. Christopher Donnellan, Rector of Inniscarra, Co. Cork, recognises the merits of the City when he describes it to Swift as a 'great Town'[88] and certainly living in the suburbs 'has all the advantages of a compleat Retirement'[89] and he gives a delightful picture of his living at Inniscarra, Co. Cork (some five miles from the City) no less true than it is to-day – 'It is a very good preferment, with at least £300 per annum... I was t'other day to view my house, and was much pleased with the situation, which is very pretty and romantic. It stands on the bank of a fine river, in a vale between two ridges of hills, that are very green, pleasant, and woody'.[90] Cork appears to have been famous for its manufacture, among other commodities, of cheese, of which it exported over five cwt. every year, and Swift appears to have known and loved Cork cheeses, as he showed when he reminded Orrery – 'I desire you will send me a present of three Cork cream Cheeses, shaped like a Sugar-Loaf. You have heard me talk of Philosopher Webber, a Cork-man, one of my Prebendryes. He hath like your Lordship an Estate in and near your Town; and some of these cheeses are sent to him: Therefore since you love Cheese, and are so good a Judge of it, I seriously expect at least six shillings worth?'[91] One last vivid, exciting picture of contemporary Cork is provided by Orrery in a letter to Swift, written in October 1735:

'There is a Custom in Corke, of which I must beg leave to inform you; with all its hideous Consequences; and to know from you whether my Behaviour has been wrong or right, that I may amend or continue it for the future according to your Decree: on the day that a new Mayor is to be chosen for this City, the black Guards assemble themselves in the High Street,[92] and come there charg'd with their Pockets full of meal and Flower, which they throw into harmless Peoples Eyes as plentifully as Beggars at Paris bestow holy water in Churches. My ill fate forc'd me from home on this important Day, and I had not gone many paces beyond the North-Gate, before a Ragged Groupe of shoe Boys blinded me in a most furious Manner with this emblem of snow. I open'd my Eyes as soon as Oat-meal and consternation would give me leave, and seeing a most despicable Sett of Wretches attacking a person for whom Mr. Hawkins the Herald has a particular Regard, I gave loose to the passions of an Irish Earl, and was going to try the sinews of my Arm and drive the ragged Regiment into the Scamander of Cork. Butt as I degenerate from my ancestors in nothing more than in their military Atchievments, Native peace returned to my natur'd Grinn, and a good-humoured Smile and pass'd on with the utmost haste, shaking my Ears and bowing at the sametime; not perhaps unlike my Dog Hector, who when he is corrected, growls, fawns and wags his Tail. The black Guards pursued me with their flowry honours, but I slipt down the first alley on my right hand, having first had the consolation to see a primitive Quaker (who had a cleaner and a finer coat on than myself) in the same Miller-like Condition'.

'These Mayoralite honours have been paid to all Christian Souls from time immemorial. The higher your rank the greater your Quantity of meal, so that if his sacred Majesty was to walk on this day from the North Gate to the South Gate in his black velvet Coat, his black Cravat and his black feather, he would only fulfil the Merlinian Prophecy of the White King'.[93]

Orrery's description of this old Cork custom is clearer from the explanation which is offered by Windele,[94] who tells us that 'formerly on the Mayor entering office, the populace enjoyed a day's saturnalia. They followed the Mayor from the Court, and flung bran upon him, in hopes of an abundant year. Hence the phrase 'bran new', but this custom as well as the old pageant of riding the franchise has long fallen into disuse'. Another writer notes that wheat and salt were thrown on the young (last) Earl of Desmond (temp. Eliz.) on his entering Kilmallock; and he cites from Pacata Hibernica, as Orrery correctly says, that this was an ancient ceremony used in the Province upon the election of Mayors and officers as a prediction of future peace and plenty.[95]

Unrepentant and unchanged in his views of Cork, it is Orrery who provides the last picture of the City. Writing from Cork, he says:

'I am going to transplant myself to Dublin. Farewell Corke! and all its' Beauties. From beef-carts I go to Privy-Counsellors, from Pilkington (a Cork Printer and Bookseller) to Faulkner and from Brocclesby to Badham. Adieu ye Kennels flowing with Bullocks Blood! Adieu ye roaring Captives in the North Gate![96] Quakers, Fools and Madmen, all adieu. My sorrowful heart is bursting. My horse stands pawing at the door. The last piece of bread and butter is in my mouth. A thousand beggars await me. I come ye limping miscreants, I come – Urbem lacrymans Portusque relinquo'.[97]

CHAPTER I

Notes

1. Lamentations, 1, 1.
2. Ibid. 2.1.2.
3. Ibid. 1. 1.
4. Quoted from *The Irish Life* (O'Curry's MS) by M. F. Cusack, *The History of Cork* p. 38 (Francis Guy, Cork, 1875).
5. *Historical and Descriptive Notices of the City of Cork* by John Windele, ed. James Coleman p. 7 (Guy & Co. Ltd. Cork, 1910) – hereinafter referred to as 'Windele'.
6. 'On Sept. 30th, 1598, the privy council wrote to the lords justices warmly urging them to appoint Spenser to that office. The letter refers to him as 'a gentleman dwelling in the County of Cork... being a man endowed with good knowledge in learning and not unskilful or without experience in the service of the wars''. Cited by Alexander C. Judson in *The Life of Edmund Spenser*, p. 200. (Baltimore: The Johns Hopkins Press, 1945).
7. *The Faerie Queene, Book IV*. Canto 11.
8. '...he died for lack of bread in King street... and refused twenty pieces sent to him by my Lord of Essex, and said he was sorry he had no time to spend them'. Cited by Alexander C. Judson, *The Life of Edmund Spenser* p. 203. Judson refers to Herford and Simpson's ed. of Jonson 1, 137, and clearly shows the improbability of this story.
9. Windele, p. 11 (supra) cites Holinshed, the English chronicler, as describing Cork in 1570 as 'Corke, in Latin Coracium or Corracium, the fourth City in Ireland, happily planted on the sea. Their haven is a haven royal...'.
10. *The Ancient and Present State of the County and City of Cork* by Charles Smith, p. 128 (Dublin 1750), hereafter cited as 'Smith'. Smith cites a very interesting letter from the Earl of Cork to Mr. Carew Raleigh, Sir Walter's son (dated at Dublin Jan. 16, 1631) in which, after describing the assistance he had given Raleigh, he adds: '...that the day he took him shipping upon his last fatal voyage from Cork, he dined with him at Sir Randal Clayton's house...'.
11. Windele (supra) p. 11, citing Holinshed.
12. Ibid. p. 11.
13. *The Council Book of the Corporation of the City of Cork*, ed. by Richard Caulfield LL.D. (J. Bellings & Sons, Surrey, 1876) p. x, cited hereafter as 'Caulfield'.
14. Caulfield, pp. x-xi.
15. Ibid. xi.
16. Ibid. xi.
17. Cocquet, or Cocket was a form of tax collection. A Cocket, originally, was a seal belonging to the King's Custom House. Later it became a sealed document delivered to merchants as a certificate that their merchandise had been duly entered

and had paid duty. It was made statutory in Cork City by 54 Geo III Cap. 196. An act to raise a fund for defraying the charge of Commercial Improvements within the City and Port of Cork, in Ireland, It was abolished by virtue of S. 183 Harbours Act 1946.

18. Caulfield, p. xi.
19. Ibid. p. xi.
20. Smith, Vol. 2, p. 33 note (b) citing Campion.
21. Caulfield, p. xii.
22. Ibid. xii.
23. Smith, Vol. 1, p. 419.
24. Caulfield, p. xii.
25. Smith, Vol. 1, p. 421.
26. Ibid.
27. Ibid.
28. *The History of the County and City of Cork* by C. B. Gibson, Vol. 1, pp. 310/317 (London, Thomas C. Henby, 1861) hereafter cited as 'Gibson'.
29. We have consulted the following works in connection with this period:
The Orrery Papers, ed. by the Countess of Cork and Orrery, 2 Vols. (London, Duckworth & Co., 1903);
The Life and Letters of the Great Earl of Cork by Dorothy Townshend (London, Duckworth & Co. 1904);
Sir Walter Raleigh in Ireland, by Sir John Pope Hennessy (London, Regan Paul, Trench & Co. 1883).
30. *The Orrery Papers*, Vol. 1, pp. xii-xiii.
31. Ibid. xvii.
32. Ibid.
33. *Remarks on the Life and Writings of Dr. Jonathan Swift*, 5th Edit. (George Faulkner, Dublin 1757).
34. *Remarks* p. 4.
35. Ibid.
36. Ibid. pp. 4-5.
37. Ibid. pp. 47/48.
38. Ibid. p. 57.
39. 'He has 3000 a year about Cork, and the neighbourhood, and has more than three years rent unpaid'; Swift to Pope, 2nd Dec. 1736. Correspondence of Jonathan Swift ed. by Harold Williams Vol. 4, p. 540 (Oxford, Clarendon Press 1965, 5 vols), hereinafter cited as 'Corr. (Williams)'.
40. Letter to Earl of Strafford from Corke, April 15th 1737. Orrery Papers, Vol. 1, p. 217.
41. Letter to Baron Waynright from Corke, April 12th 1737. Ibid. p. 215.
42. Ibid.
43. Ibid. p. 216.
44. See Chapter 6.
45. Lord Orrery to Swift, Corke March 15th 1736/37 'Corr. (Williams)' Vol. 5. p. 9.
46. *The Orrery Papers*, Vol. 1, p. 120.
47. Ibid. p. 206. Letter to Thomas Southerne from Corke, March 20th 1736.
48. Letter to Dean Brandreth 30th June 1732. Corr. (Williams) Vol. 4, p. 34.
49. Ibid.
50. Ibid. pp. 34/35.

51. Ibid. p. 34.
52. Ibid.
53. *Jonathan Swift and Ireland* by Oliver W. Ferguson, p. 7 (University of Illinois Press, Urbana 1962) hereafter cited as 'Ferguson'.
54. *England Under Queen Anne: The Peace and the Protestant Succession*, p. 181, by G. M. Trevelyan (The Fontana Library, 1965).
55. Ibid.
56. Ibid, pp. 182/183.
57. Gibson, Vol. 2, p. 201.
58. Caulfield, p. 294.
59. Ibid. p. 319.
60. Ibid.
61. Ibid. pp. 335/336.
62. Letter to Anexander Pope, May 2nd 1730. Corr. (Williams) Vol. 3, p. 394.
63. *Journal to Stella*, Letter 5, Vol. 1 p. 45 (Oxford, Clarendon Press) hereafter cited as 'Journal'.
64. Journal, Letter 39, pp. 464/465.
65. Ibid.
66. *My Irish Journal*, 1669-1670 by William Penn, p. 13, ed. Isabel Grubb (Longman, Green & Co. 1952): Gibson (Vol. 2 p. 133) reminds us that there is no such text in the Bible, and suggests that the text used was from the Epistle of St. John ch. 5: 4 – 'This is the victory that overcometh the world, even our faith'.
67. Ibid.
68. Ibid. p. 14.
69. Caulfield, p. 210.
70. Ibid. p. 211.
71. *My Irish Journal* pp. 14/15.
72. See n. 45.
73. Corr. (Williams) Vol. 2, p. 141.
74. *England under Queen Anne* (supra) p. 193.
75. Caulficld, p. 318/319.
76. Ibid.
77. Ferguson, p. 17.
78. Ibid.
79. Ibid. p. 18.
80. *The Early Irish Stage*, by William Smith Clark, p. 137. (Oxford, Clarenden Press, 1955) hereafter cited as 'Clark'.
81. Ibid.
82. Caulfield, p. 340.
83. Smith, Vol. 1, p. 401. 'The Exchange, which almost divides the main street in the City into two parts N. and S. is an handsome regular structure of hewn stone. The front consists of five arches, with three others next the passage to the street. The middle arch or principal entrance is adorned with columns of the Doric order, over which are fluted ones of Ionic order; between the front windows are pilasters of the same, with an handsome cornice or balustrade over these. On the top is an elegant cupola covered with lead, a gilt ball, cross and dragon'.
84. *Irish Life in the Sevententh Century*, ed. MacLysaght (London, 1939).
85. Smith, Vol. 1, p. 407.
86. *English Goldsmiths and Their Marks* (Second Edition) by Sir Charles J. Jackson, pp. 680/681 (Macmillans).

87. Smith, Vol. 1 pp. 411/413.
88. Rev. Christopher Donnellan to Swift, Corke July 2nd, 1736. Corr. (Williams) Vol. 4 p. 510.
89. Ibid. 510.
90. Ibid. 413.
91. Swift to Lord Orrery, 31st March 1737. Corr. (Williams) Vol. 5, p. 23.
92. 'The High Street, called here the Main Street, is intermixed with old and new buildings, and as the former decay new ones rise in the modern taste. Most of these houses have balcony windows in the Spanish fashion and are built of brick'. Smith, Vol. 1, pp. 407/408.
93. Lord Orrery to Swift, Oct. 1735. Corr. (Williams) Vol. 4, p. 401.
94. Windele, p. 63.
95. James Buckley in *The Orrery Papers*. Journal of Cork Archeological and Historical Society,Vol. 9, p. 237, hereafter cited as 'J.C.A.H.S.'
96. A reference to the South and North Gates or entrances to the walled City of Cork, and at which prisoners were kept.
97. Earl of Orrery to John Kempe, Cork, Nov. 18th, 1736. *The Orrery Papers* Vol. 1. pp. 175/176.

'I am forced to leave the town sooner than I expected'

Dr. Samuel Johnson did not, particularly, care for Swift, as a man. 'He seemed to me to have an unaccountable prejudice against Swift; for I once took the liberty to ask him, if Swift had personally offended him, and he told me he had not. He said to-day, 'Swift is clear, but he is shallow. In coarse humour, he is inferior to Arbuthnot; in delicate humour he is inferior to Addison. So he is inferior to his contemporaries; without putting him against the world...''.[1] Yet, in his account of Swift's association with Vanessa, he is more than fair to Swift, and less than fair to Vanessa:

'In 1723 died Mrs Van Homrigh, a woman made unhappy by her admiration of wit and ignominiously distinguished by the name of Vanessa whose conduct has been already sufficiently discussed, and whose history is too well known to be minutely repeated. She was a young woman fond of literature, whom Decanus, the Dean, called Cadenus by transposition of the letters, took pleasure in directing and instructing; till, from being proud of his praise, she grew fond of his person. Swift was then about forty-seven, at an age when vanity is strongly excited by the amorous attention of a young woman. If it should be said that Swift should have checked a passion which he never meant to gratify, recourse must be had to that extenuation which he so much despised, 'men are but men'; perhaps, however, he did not at all first know his own mind, and, as he represents himself, was undetermined. For his admission of her courtship, and his indulgence of her hopes after his marriage to Stella, no other honest plea can be found than that he delayed a disagreeable discovery from time to time, dreading the immediate bursts of distress, and watching for a favourable moment. She thought herself neglected and died of disappointment; having ordered by her will the poem to be published, in which Cadenus had proclaimed her excellence, and confessed his love. The effect of publication upon... Stella is thus related by Delaney:... 'as the poem of Cadenus and Vanessa was then the general topic of conversation, one of them said, 'surely Vanessa must be an extraordinary woman, that could inspire the dean to write so finely upon her', Mrs Johnson smiled and answered, 'that she thought that point not quite so clear; for it was well known the dean could write finely upon a broomstick''.[2]

Yet, in spite of Johnson, and in spite of Stella, Swift could write of her –

> 'Then sows within her tender mind
> Seeds long unknown to womankind,
> For manly Bosoms chiefly fit,
> The Seeds of Knowledge, Judgment, Wit.
> Her Soul was suddenly endu'd
> With Justice, Truth and Fortitude;
> With Honour, which no breath can stain,
> Which Malice must attack in vain;
> With open Heart and bounteous Hand' ...[3]

whilst denying that on his side there was any declaration of love –

> 'And Cupid hop'd they wou'd improve
> By time, and ripen into love
>
> . . . .
>
> Cadenus warded off the Blows
> For Placing still some Book betwixt,
> The Darts were in the Cover fix'd[4]

while she, in despair, could plead

> 'Oh, Pallas! I invoke thy aid!
> Vouchsafe to hear a wretched maid
>   By tender love deprest;
> 'Tis just that thou should'st heal the smart
> Inflicted by thy subtle art,
>   And calm my troubled breast...[5]

and she could pour out her heart with longing – 'Cad., is it possible that you will come and see me, I beg for God sake you will I would give the world to see you here...'6 and again, 'Tell me sincerely if you have once wished with earnestness to see me since I wrote to you. No so far from that you have not once pity'd me though I told you how I was distressed solitude is insupportable to a mind which is not easie I have worn out my days in sighing and my nights with watching and thinking of –, –, –, – – –, who thinks not of me how many letters must I send you before I shall receive an answer can you deny me in my misery the only comfort which I can expect at present...'7 and in her frenzy she knew him, perhaps, better than anyone who had ever known him, when she wrote – 'I firmly believe could I know your thoughts (which no humane creature is capable of geussing at because never any one liveing thought like you...'8 and, when the end came, with Swift riding to Celbridge like 'a black intimidating thundercloud under a lowering sky',9 confronting Vanessa in cold, implacable silence, flinging her letter to Stella on to a table, turning on his heel and leaving her life for ever, it was inevitable that she would die, very shortly, sick as she was with a consumption which had killed so many of her family, and broken with shock and shame.

Swift may or may not have considered the necessity of flight, in the event of Vanessa's death. Her illness was known to him. Its ultimate fatal end could not have been outside his purview. The consequences of his final visit to her must, surely, have occurred to him, if not prior to, then at least subsequent to it. Whether his southern journey was planned before or after his rupture with Vanessa is not as difficult to determine as the possibility that the one was planned to follow the other. If it was not, then it certainly had the appearance of pre-arrangement. 'Most of the fog is the deliberate work of Swift himself, and how delighted he must be – wherever he is – to observe that after two hundred years, the fog is still billowing around him'.10 Obviously, if his departure was considered, as a consequence of his break with Vanessa, apart from the consequences of gossip, he would have considered placing as great a distance between them as was possible. As well as this, secrecy was called for, and it would be necessary to remain away from Dublin for as long as he, conveniently, could do so, and until the gossip had died down. What happened was not, perhaps, the way Swift had planned. Vanessa's death was sudden. Sheridan's account of what followed is, briefly, expressed:

'Swift, on receiving tidings of her death, immediately took horse and quitted the town, without letting any mortal know to what part of the world he was gone. As he foresaw that this event would give rise to much town-talk he thought it most prudent to keep out of the way, till the first heat of it was over. And having never visited the Southern part of the Kingdom, he took this opportunity of making a tour there, because having no acquaintance in those parts he might be a perfect master of his own motions, and in his solitary rambles give free vent to his grief for the loss of so beloved an object, heightened by the bitter aggravation of knowing himself to be the cause of her death. Two months had elapsed without any news of him, which occasioned no small alarm among his friends; when Mr. Sheridan received a letter from him, to meet him at a certain distance from Dublin'.[11]

It would be an understatement to describe this highly coloured account as containing several inaccuracies and distortions of fact. The pity of it is that later biographers followed Sheridan's account, and Sir Walter Scott, shamelessly, paraphrases Sheridan as follows: 'Upon the death of Miss Vanhomrigh, Swift in an agony of self-reproach, retreated into the South of Ireland, where he spent two months, without the place of his abode being known to anyone'.[12] The fact is that Swift had, already, fixed the date of a Southern tour. Proof of this is contained in a letter which he wrote to Robert Cope on May 11th 1723 – 'I will tell you that for some years I have intended a Southern journey; and this Summer is fixed for it, and I hope to set out in ten days',[13] that is about May 21st. At the same time, Swift left no doubt, and certainly none to Vanessa, of his desire to avoid disputes and quarrels with her – 'We differ prodigiously in one point, I fly from the spleen to the world's end. You run out of your way to meet it'.[14] If Swift was intent upon providing evidence that he had decided to leave Dublin before any final break with Vanessa had taken place, he does so for the second time in yet another letter which 'I wrote to you three weeks ago; perhaps my letter miscarried. I desire you would let Dr. Jenney know that I intended my journey in ten days after my letter would reach you; and I staid five or six more, and do now leave this town on Monday';[15] that is, June 1st. The final break between Swift and Vanessa occurred 'on a late Spring day in the year 1723'.[16] Following upon it, Vanessa made her will. It is dated May 1st 1723. Vanessa died on June 2nd 1723. It appears to have been a carefully considered testament which must have taken some days to prepare. There are nineteen specific bequests of money which are to be expended on the purchase of mourning rings, a custom which in those days was very common. There is no indication of any distress or emotion, no hint or note of recrimination: The only unusual feature of the will is the appointment of stranger executors. One of these was George Berkeley, the famous philosopher who was later to be appointed Bishop of Cloyne, Co. Cork. The other was Robert Marshall, a young lawyer, later to become a Justice of the Court of Common Pleas and upon whom on March, 20th 1748 was conferred the Freedom of Cork.[17] One may conjecture that, before instructing her lawyers to draw her will, Vanessa must have sent for Dr. Berkeley and Robert Marshall, made known to them her wishes, and revealed the conditions upon which the residue of her estate was being bequeathed to Berkeley. It is suggested that this condition was that her executors were to agree to publish the correspondence which had passed between herself and Swift. 'The Archbishop of Dublin must have been extremely perturbed to hear from the Rev. Dr. Sheridan that Mrs Van Homrigh, recently dead, had left her executors instructions to publish letters which had passed between herself and the Dean of St. Patricks'.[18] Some further evidence that Swift's departure was a planned one is provided by the fact that at or about the same time Stella, accompanied by her companion Rebecca Dingley, left Dublin and remained away for about six months at Woodpark, the residence of Swift's friend Charles Ford –

> 'Don Carlos in a merry spight
> Did Stella to his house invite:
> He entertained her half a year
> With gen'rous Wines and costly chear'.[19]

Sir Harold Williams identifies the Don Carlos of the poem as Charles Ford, and says, 'If the 'half a year' of l. 3 is to be taken literally, Stella's visit to Woodpark in 1723 extended from April to October, for we know from the title of Stella's distress that she returned to Dublin on 3rd October'.[20] It is a feature of these missing months that the man who wrote so regularly to Stella, on other occasions upon which he was separated from her, never so much as wrote her a single line during this particular absence, and that Stella accepted it, so far as we know, without demur. This may be indicative of some agreement between them as to the necessity for silence as to his movements or whereabouts. Indeed, while Swift was away from Dublin only two letters appear to have been written by him.[21] The claim that Sheridan received a letter from him two months after his departure from Dublin suggesting they should meet 'at a certain distance from Dublin' is, manifestly and in fact, the product of Sheridan's imagination, since Swift remained away some four months, and no such letter has ever been discovered. Reverting to the reasons for our view that Swift had decided both to break with Vanessa and upon doing so to leave Dublin, it is submitted that Vanessa was, at that time, determined to force a decision from Swift; that she had written Stella – what she said we do not know (it was sufficient to drive the Dean into a terrible rage). It is possible, also, either that the Archbishop of Dublin had been consulted by Swift in his dilemma, or had summoned Swift and advised him to leave Dublin. Sheridan seems to suggest to the contrary – 'Sheridan assured the Archbishop that neither his clergy nor his friends had the least idea where he had gone, and were, therefore, unable to make contact'.[22] At least one person, Robert Cope, knew; because, in the course of his letters to him, Swift said that from the South he intended to go on to the Bishop of Clonfert. One thing is reasonably certain, and that is that the Archbishop threw all his power and influence behind Swift in order to protect him and kill the scandal. The Bishop of Meath wrote to a friend – 'Ye Archbishop of Dublin and ye whole Irish posse have (I fear) prevailed with Mr. Marshall (ye lady's executor) not to print the papers etc., as she desired lest one of their own joyes should be trampled on by the Philistines'.[23] But Swift, with what was his usual strategy, was determined not to leave himself open to the suggestion that he had 'run away', or was in hiding without leaving some information as to his whereabouts. That is why, as it seems to us, he insisted on informing Robert Cope that he intended to go South and thereafter on to the Bishop of Clonfert. He made it clear, furthermore – 'I was never in these parts, nor am acquainted with one Christian among them'.[24] We know, now, that Swift went to the Parish of Myross in the Barony of Carbery, which is situated in the western tip of the County of Cork. Here we may refer to some confusion which has been created by Sheridan in his *Life*. In one statement, he asserts that Swift had, previously, visited Cork and had been entertained by the Cork Corporation:

'Swift, like many who jest freely on others, could not bear a retort. During one day at a public dinner of the Mayor and Corporation at Corke, he observed that Alderman Brown, father to the Bishop of that diocese, fed very heartily without speaking a word, and was so intent upon that business, as to become a proper object of ridicule. Accordingly he threw out many successful jests upon the Alderman, who fed on with the silence of the still sow, neither seeming to regard what the Dean said, nor at all moved by the repeated burst of laughter, at his expense. Toward the latter end of the meal, Swift happened to be helped to some roasted duck, and desired to have some apple sauce on the same plate; upon which the Alderman bawled out, 'Mr. Dean, you eat your duck like a goose'. This unexpected sally threw the Company into a long continued fit of laughter, and Swift was silent the rest of the day'.

If this incident took place, which we doubt, and our doubt is shared by the view of no less an authority than Dr. Elrington Ball who, in Volume Three of his monumental edition of the correspondence, suggests that this particular anecdote is not unknown, and that in the Midlands Counties Historical Collector I. 59, the same jest has been attributed to a Leicester gentleman, it could only have taken place on one specific occasion in 1725, that is upon the occasion of Rev. Thomas Sheridan's induction as Rector of Rincurran, Kinsale, Co. Cork, at which, in a later portion of this work, we suggest there is some very slight evidence to suggest Swift attended. The most likely source of this anecdote is the Rev. Thomas Sheridan himself. The Bishop Brown referred to was Peter Brown, who was consecrated Bishop of Cork in 1710, and died at Bishopstown, Co. Cork, in 1735, and upon whose career we offer some observations later in this work. We shall, furthermore, suggest that Swift was known to several Cork and Cork County personages, with whom he was on terms of friendship and familiarity. Bishop Brown was one, the Rev. Philip Townsend was another, and the Earl of Orrery was possibly, his closest Cork associate. There is an apparent contradiction in Sheridan's statements; because on the one hand he cites the anecdote above referred to, and on the other, asserts that 'Swift had never visited the Southern part of the Kingdom'. He does not specifically say that he had never visited Cork. The similarity of the words used with those used by Swift in his letter to Robert Cope raises two possibilities, either that Robert Cope had shown Rev. Thomas Sheridan Swift's letters to him, and Sheridan Senr. had so informed his son – a possibility which we discount, or Thomas Sheridan when writing Swift's life had read Swift's correspondence, first published by George Faulkener. The Rev. Thomas Sheridan became Rector of

Rincurran on July 2nd, 1725. There was no reason why the Cork Corporation should have honoured Rev. Thomas Sheridan with a Dinner. Examination of the Records of the Cork Corporation shows that the Lord Mayor, Aldermen and Councillors were not averse to holding celebrations on every occasion which was or seemed important. Such celebrations were, always, recorded, as they called for the expenditure of Corporation funds. The year 1725 saw three celebrations – '14th May 1725: That £12 be allowed for an entertainment at the Tholsell on the King's birthday:[25] 22nd July 1725: That £10 be appointed for an entertainment on 1 Aug. next;[26] 11th Oct. 1725: That £10 be paid for an entertainment on the King's Coronation'.[27] If Swift was entertained to dinner by the Cork Corporation, the most likely date would have been 1st August 1725, which was for a purpose which is not stated in the records. On the other hand, Swift himself, in a letter to the Earl of Oxford, dated Aug. 14th 1725, provides evidence for the fact that for four months prior to his letter he had been 'in a little obscure Irish cabinn about fourty miles from Dublin, whither I fled to avoyd Company in frequent returns of deafness'.[28] There is one piece of evidence which, if we interpret it correctly, would suggest the possibility that Swift was, at some time, in Cork. This is provided by Swift himself, in a letter which he wrote Rev. Thomas Sheridan following upon the latter's presentation to the living of Rincurran, Co. Cork. Sheridan's letters of presentation were dated July 2nd, and his institution was to take place on July 19th. Swift was then staying at Sheridan's home at Quilca, Co. Cavan. Sheridan had written Swift, presumably from Cork. This letter is not available to us. We know, however, from Swift's reply, that he had written Swift on 'tomorrow, June 29th', [29] and it may be that he asked Swift to come to Co. Cork for the induction ceremony. In the course of his answer, Swift acknowledging, says – 'Therefore your own mare and Dr. S – horse or mare, or some other horse or mare, with your own mare aforesaid, shall set out on Wednesday next, which will be June 30th and so they will have two nights rest, if you begin your journey on Saturday'.[30] In his letters to Robert Cope, Swift does not say that he had never been in the City of Cork – but merely 'I never was in those parts', that is in that part of the County to which he intended to travel. The suggestion that he was not 'acquainted with one Christian among them' is not borne out by the fact that when writing Thomas Sheridan he says – 'Mr. Townshend of Cork will do you any good offices on my account'.[31] In our view, the 'Mr. Townshend' referred to in that letter was Rev.

Philip Townsend, sixth son of Colonel Richard Townsend of Castle-townshend, who was born in 1664 at Kilbrittain Castle, near Timoleague, Co. Cork, and entered Trinity College Dublin as a pensioner on 20th June 1684. He, at first adopted the military profession, and was a captain in the army, but subsequently entered into Holy Orders, and in 1706 was admitted by Bishop Dive Downes to the Prebend of Lisclery, and by Bishop Crow of Cloyne to the R.V. of Aghinagh, in Cloyne. These livings, together with the important vicarage of the Holy Trinity, Cork, which he received in 1707, he held until his death. Now, Professor Irwin Ehrenpreis has established that Swift and his cousin Thomas proceeded to Trinity College as Pensioners on April 24th 1682.[32] Prof. Ehrenpreis also shows that Swift was still a student at Trinity in 1685, 1686 and 1687, and he cites a letter written by Swift in 1692 saying that he had spent seven years at Trinity, which would place his departure as in or about the Spring of 1689 or probably earlier. Thus, Swift and Townshend being members of the Trinity Divinity School would have known each other for several years and, probably, were on terms of friendship. That he was, sufficiently, acquainted with the Bishop of Cork[33] to address him on Sheridan's behalf is clear from what Prof. Ehrenpreis says on the subject of Swift's associates – 'Since the Administrative class, to which Swift belonged, was to be numbered in the hundreds, there could be few of them whom he would not meet sooner or later… he was bound to find at Trinity College many people who would remain his acquaintances in later years. It could hardly be otherwise, for in Ireland any Protestant of Swift's generation who did take a University Degree was more likely to choose Trinity College than Oxford or Cambridge'.[34] Ehrenpreis also points out that Browne was admitted to Trinity College less than two months after Swift, and took his B.A. degree at the same time.

We return now to the events which followed the announcement of Vanessa's death. Once again, Swift, notwithstanding the suddenness of her demise, is careful to ensure that there can be no question of 'flight' being charged against him, and that he was doing no more than advancing the date of a tour already arranged. That he was taken unawares, however, is quite clear as he writes to his friend Knightly Chetwode 'past twelve at midnight',[35] and confesses 'I am forced to leave the Town sooner than I expected'.[36] If there is no sign of panic, there are obvious signs of strain, disquiet and apprehension, and a remarkable and unusual insight in Swift's assessment of what public opinion may be – 'It is worse to need friends than not to have them; especially in times when it is so hard, even for cautious men to keep out of harm's way'.[37] And so he rides away and there is silence – a silence which continued for three months and not, as Sheridan says, for two months, when Swift writes to Rev. Thomas Sheridan from Clonfert, Co. Galway, saying – 'No, I cannot possibly be with you so soon, there are too many Rivers, Bogs, and Mountains between; besides, when I leave this I shall make one or two short visits in my way to Dublin and hope to be in Town by the end of the month'.[38] Does not this suggest that Sheridan knew Swift's itinerary would take him to the Bishop of Clonfert, and that instead of Swift having written him, within two months of his departure, asking for a meeting at a certain distance from Dublin, it is more likely that Sheridan sent a letter addressed to Swift at Clonfert suggesting that they could meet some distance from Dublin? Sheridan's close friendship with Swift qualified him, more than any other, to communicate the gossip and happenings in Dublin following Vanessa's death, and Swift's departure. Swift, however, did not want to know, and would make his own way back to Dublin in his own time.

When Swift left Dublin, he rode South to County Cork. His route is unknown. The veil of silence which covers this part of his life is not easily lifted. It is certain that he made his way to the Parish of Myross, which is situated on the West side of Glandore Harbour, in the Barony of Carbery. Carbery was the largest Barony in Ireland. Its beauty surpasses description. It was not, easily, accessible. It is more than likely that Swift's route brought him through Cashel, Co. Tipperary, where he may have stayed at the Bishop's Palace, and then gone on to Cork, where he would meet several of his friends. Then he would ride from Cork to Bandon, a distance of twenty one miles, a further thirteen miles to Clonakilty, a town which was incorporated by the interest of the first Earl of Cork and governed by a Sovereign and Burgesses. The list of towns and Protestant families in that area is worthy of note. Smith refers to Palace-Anne, six miles west of Bandon where Roger Bernard lived in his 'handsome large well built house, Palace Anne... on the south side of the Bandon river is Warrensbrook... of Mr. Warren. Two miles more west... is Connorsville, the house and seat of William Connor Esq.... on the other side of the river is Pheal, a good house of Mr. Wade. Twelve miles west of Bandon was Dunmanway, the seat of Sir Richard Cox.[39] Not far from Clonakilty was Rosscarbery, and clustered around were Banduff, Glandore, Leap, Myross, Squince Island, Castlehaven, formerly called Glanbarahane, Castle-

Townshend, seat of Col. Bryan Townshend. Tradition has it that Swift did stay in Bandon on his way to Myross, and there saw inscribed on its walls the famous lines – 'A Turk, a Jew, or an Atheist may live in this Town, but no Papist'.[40] Tuckey cites it as a fact, and the Countess of Orrery adds to Tuckey's view. It is also said that when Swift saw these lines, he added the following couplet –

'He that wrote these lines did write them well,
As the same is written on the gates of hell'.

George Bennett[41] agrees that Swift spent some time in Bandon; but does not give the source of his information. Bennett insists that no such inscription ever appeared on the walls of Bandon, and gives the year in which Swift stayed there as 1729,[42] which, of course, could not be correct. He claimed to have been favoured with 'the only copy extant' of the entire poem which we transcribe hereunder:

'A Turk, a Jew, or an Atheist,
May live in this town, but no Papist.
He that wrote these lines did write them well,
As the same is written on the gates of hell
For Friar Hayes, who made his exit of late,
Of some say. But, no matter for that.
He died; and, if what we've heard is aright,
He came to hells gates in a mournful plight.
'Who's there'? says the sentry on guard. Quoth the other,
'A wretched poor priest, sir, a Catholic brother'.
'Halt! instantly halt! Avaunt! and stay clear;
Go be damned somewhere else; you shan't be damned here;
We admit no such fellow, for a wretch so uncivil,
Who on earth would eat God, would in hell eat the Devil'.[43]

The second couplet might well have been written by Swift; but, so also, might it have been written by any other caustic wit. Sir Harold Williams' standard edition of Swift's poems makes no claim to authorship by Swift of these lines.

We must now return to several slightly varying accounts of Swift's activities in Myross. First, we refer to the statement contained in *An Officer of the Long Parliament*[44] – 'It was at this period that Dean Swift spent some time in West Carbery. He stayed at Myross', but there is some uncertainty with whom he stayed. On the other hand, it seems reasonably probable that the house at which he lived is identified. First, then, we have Smith's account, which is as follows: Some years ago the Revd Dean Swift spent a summer at a clergymans house (since also dead) in the Parish of Miros; he often diverted himself in making little voyages on the coast from Glandore Harbour towards Baltimore; and these excursions occasioned his Latin poem called *Carberia Rupes*.[45] There are several interesting features about Smith's statement in relation to Swift. Smith's work was written prior to Nov. 6th 1727, on which date a manuscript copy was laid before the Board of the Physico-Historical Society, the Vice-Presidence of which was Ed. Barry M.D. who was one and the same person as the Ed. Barry M.D. who was so close a friend and confidant of John Earl of Orrery, to whom the work was dedicated. We refer in another part of this work (Chap. 3) to Edward Barry's assessment of Swift. It is interesting also to note among the subscribers to the works, the names of several of Swift's contemporaries, including Rt. Rev. George Berkeley, Lord Bishop of Cloyne, Ed. Barry, Rt. Hon. John, Earl of Orrery, Rt. Hon. Edward Southwell, and several other Cork names such as Columbine Lee Carrée, son of Augustus Carrée; who dissented from the motion to confer the Freedom of Cork on Swift, and such chroniclers as Rev. Richard Pococke LL.D., Archdeacon of Dublin, whose diary of an extensive tour of the South of Ireland, and covering much of the country in which Swift must have travelled, is preserved in the Journal of the Cork Archeological and Historical Society. In these circumstances, therefore, Smith must be credited with having first-hand information of the facts. The great pity is that he does not identify the clergyman with whom Swift stayed. Another account, published in 1892,[46] suggests that his friend, Rev. R. Somerville, was then Rector of Myross, an assertion which, for the reasons following, we reject. The same account adds – 'It is most likely the Protestant congregation of Myross, in the time Dean Swift visited the Rector was considerable – the familiar (names) of Somerville, Lyster, Townshend, French and others' being among them. Again, there is some confusion here; because according to Brady,[47] Rev. George Synge A.B. was admitted Rector and Vicar of Myross in 1706, and held this office until 1732.[48] Furthermore, we cannot find any reference to a Rev. R. Somerville in Brady but there is a reference to Rev. Thomas Somerville

A.M., who was admitted to the Rectorship and Vicarage of Myross on Feb. 16th 1732/3 following on the death of Rev. George Synge.[49] Thomas Somerville was the son of Rev. William Somerville, and was born in Scotland. When he was seventeen years old, he entered Trinity College, Dublin, as a Pensioner, on 30th October 1706. He was ordained Priest on 1st November 1715 at Cloyne. From 1719-1724 he was Rector of Killanully, and also, probably, curate of Holy Trinity, Cork, to which he was licensed on 2nd Nov. 1721. From 1724 to 1732 he was priest at Caherlag, and from 1732 to his death in 1752 he was Rector and Vicar at Myross. It is less than likely, therefore, that Rev. R. Somerville or Rev. Thomas Somerville, received Swift in Myross in June 1723. The two most likely hosts are Rev. George Synge or Rev. Philip Somerville. Records of the Somerville family contain the following notes – 'It was at this period that Dean Swift spent some time in West Carbery. He stayed at Myross, but is said to have written his poem Carberiae Rupes in a ruined tower at Castle Townshend, still known as Swift's Tower. It is also said that letters from the great Dean are still preserved at Castle Townshend and that he named one of the houses in the village 'Laputa'.[50] 'Laputa' is identified as Glen Barrahane, the seat of Sir C. J. Coghill Bart. Edith Somerville and Martin Ross in their book *Irish Memories* repeat the Somerville tradition, without asserting that any letters of the Dean are preserved at Castle Townshend. No such letters are cited in Williams, and the source of the learned editors' information is given as the manuscript work of a Mr. G. Digby Daunt. One further source of information available is that provided in Samuel Lewis,[51] who at that time described Myross as 'a Parish in the Eastern Division of the Barony of West Carbery, County of Cork, and Province of Munster, 6 miles (S.W. by W.) from Ross; containing with the village of Union Hall 3459 inhabitants... Myross Wood, the demesne of F. H. Coppinger Esq., is very large extending northwards to the Leap... Clantaafe is the residence of R. Townsend Esq. Bunlahan of Major Powell; Brade of the Rev. E. P. Thompson; Union Hall of Capt. Somerville; Ballincolla, of Capt. Lyster; and Rock Cottage of J. French, Esq.,... At Rock Cottage, now the residence of J. French Esq., Dean Swift wrote his poem of *Carberiae Rupes*'.[52]

Carberiae Rupes is a Latin poem which has become famous because of its accurate and powerful description of a local scene, and also because of an equally brilliant rendering from the pen of Rev. Dr. Dunkin, that same minister who, gratuitously, intervened in the dispute between Swift and

Richard Bettesworth, with which we shall deal in Chapter Five, and without any personal reason lampooned him as scornfully as did Swift.

Smith makes the following observations relating to the poem – "'Hinc atq.' etc. This alludes to a stupendous arch through which a boat may row. It is in the Parish of Miros and not far from the place where the Dean usually embarked. Near the West head of Castlehaven are deep caves which are low at the entrance, but grow higher within. The swell of the sea raises a boat up to the roof almost when one is in, which also by turns closes up the entrance and makes them very dark and gloomy'.

Nothing more is known of this period in the Dean's life. If the Dean is responsible for most of the fog, it is hard to understand the apparent lack of any family or other written records among the people with whom he lived. We must, for the moment, accept this. At the end of four months he returned to Dublin, and very dryly and laconicly writes to his friend Alexander Pope explaining his absence – 'Returning from a Summer expedition of four months on account of health found a letter from you…'.[53] The iron, however, has eaten into Swift's soul, and he allows himself to ruminate on the difference between Friendship and Love – 'for a Lover (as I have heard) is always scribbling to his Mistress'.[55] That he has suffered he indicates with – 'Non sum qualis eram: I left you in a period of life where one year does more Execution than three at yours, to which if you add the dullness of the Air and of the People it will make a terrible Sermon'.[55] Perhaps, too, he had good reason to ponder on words which Alexander Pope had written him in August 1723 – 'Consider there is One to whom you yourself have been as great a Sinner'.[56]

46

Notes

1. Boswell's *Life of Johnson* ed. George Birbeck Hill, Vol. 5, p. 44. (Oxford: Clarendon Press 1934, Six Vols.).
2. *Lives of the Poets* – Samuel Johnson (The Fontana Library, ed. 1963) pp. 315/316.
3. *Poems of Jonathan Swift*, ed. Harold Williams (Second Edition) Vol. II p. 693 ll. 202-210 (Oxford: Clarendon Press 1958), hereafter cited as 'Poems'.
4. Ibid. ll. 474-475; 479-481.
5. *Ode To Wisdom*: cited in *The Works Of The English Poets*, Vol. XI p. 398. (London 1810).
6. Corr. (Williams) Vol. 2, p. 357.
7. Ibid. pp. 363-364.
8. Ibid. p. 364.
9. *In Search of Swift*, Denis Johnston, p. 3. (Hodges Figgis, Dublin 1959).
10. Ibid. p. 9.
11. Life of Swift, p. 289.
12. *The Works of Jonathan Swift D.D.* (1814) Vol. 1 p. 259.
13. Corr. (Williams) Vol. 2, p. 453.
14. Ibid. p. 429.
15. Ibid. p. 455.
16. *In Search of Swift*, p. 3.
17. Robert Marshall was the son of John Marshall of Clonmel Co. Tipperary. He became a member of Parliament, a sergeant-at-law, and a Justice of the Court of Common Pleas. See 'Robert Marshall of Clonmel' by F. Elrington Ball M.R.I.A. in J.C.H.A.S. 2nd series vol. 3, no 31-33, p. 263.
18. *Cadenus* by Sybil Le Brocquy, p. 107 (The Dolmen Press, Dublin 1962).
19. Poems, Vol. 2, p. 749.
20. Ibid. p. 748.
21. Aug. 3rd 1723 from Clonfert to Thomas Sheridan, and Sept. 20th 1723, upon his return to Dublin, to Alexander Pope.
22. Life of Swift.
23. Bishop of Meath to the Archbishop of Cantebury, cited by Sybil Le Brocquy, ibid. at p. 43/44.
24. Corr. (Williams) Vol. 2, p. 453.
25. Caulfield, p. 454.
26. Ibid. p. 455.
27. Ibid. p. 457.
28. Corr. (Williams) Vol. 3, p. 84.
29. Ibid. p. 66.
30. Ibid.

31. Ibid. p. 67.
32. *Swift – The Man, His Works And The Age* (Vol. 1) by Irwin Ehrenpreis (Methuen & Co. 1962).
33. Dr. Peter Browne.
34. Ehrenpreis, supra, at p. 71.
35. Corr. (Williams) Vol. 2, p. 457.
36. Ibid.
37. Ibid.
38. Ibid. Vol. 2, p. 463.
39. Smith, Vol. 1, p. 261.
40. The Countess of Cork and Orrery sets up a claim in the name of Roger, Lord Broghill, first Earl of Orrery, for this composition. She writes – 'Earl Roger having proved throughout his career a Protestant of somewhat aggressive staunchness, whereby he is credited with the incident of having inscribed the gates of the town of Bandon Bridge with the following Distich –

> 'Jew, Infidel, or Atheist
> May enter here, but not a Papist'.

The Orrery Papers, Vol. 1. XIII.

41. *The History of Bandon* by George Bennett, p. 303. (Cork, Henry and Coghlan, 1862).
42. Ibid. p. 303.
43. Ibid. p. 304.
44. Ed. by Richard and Dorothea Townshend (London, Henry Froude) Oxford University Press 1892.
45. Poems: Vol. 1, p. 315.
46. John R. O'Flanagan in J.C.A.H.S. Vol. IA, p. 144-145.
47. Clerical and Parochial Records of Cork, Cloyne and Ross by W. Maziere Brady D.D. (Alexander Thom, Dublin, 1873).
48. Ibid. p. 536.
49. Ibid.
50. An Officer of the Long Parliament, supra.
51. *A Topographical Dictionary of Ireland* (London 1837).
52. Ibid.
53. Corr. (Williams) Vol 2, p. 464.
54. Ibid.
55. Ibid.
56. Corr. (Williams) Vol. 2, p. 460.

St. Peter's Church, Cork

CHAPTER THREE

'Sufficient unto the day is the evil therereof'

'An eighteenth-century clergyman, as a matter of course, kept a watchful eye on the health of any of his brethren whose benefices were worth coveting; and as the incumbent of... lay dying, the potential successors and those empowered to dispose of the benefice, Swift included, began to lay plans'.[1] These words, while of general application, were written of a particular incumbency in Dublin. They might, equally have applied to the Rectorship of Rincurran, Kinsale, Co. Cork, which became vacant in 1724 following the death of John Francis, the then Rector.[2] No sooner was Francis dead than the various candidates began soliciting the help of powerful friends. So, we read in the Council Book of Kinsale under date May 11, 1725, a letter addressed to Southwell by Rev. John Blair, which is worth quoting:

'The Bishop of Limerick is dead; no doubt Dr. Burscough will be recommended to that see. I think your answer from Mr. Secretary Clutterbuck was that, if Burscough was provided for, Rincurran should be given to your recommendation. Now, as you were so good as to recommend me, I beg you to insist upon the promise made you. I have no friend beside your Honour but the Abp of Dublin; whose interest at present is not very good. My long services will, I hope, move you to endeavour to procure a settlement for a poor wandering Clergyman that hath been three and twenty years in the Crown service'.[3]

At the same time, Swift was keenly interested in obtaining the appointment for his friend Thomas Sheridan. Sheridan, the son of Patrick Sheridan, a gentleman who possessed a small estate near Kilmore, in Cavan, was a near relative of Patrick Sheridan, Bishop of Cloyne, and of William Sheridan, his brother, Bishop of Kilmore. By the help of the Bishop of Kilmore, Sheridan, when twenty years of age, was enabled to enter T.C.D. as a

Pensioner on 18th October 1707, and subsequently attained the D.D. degree in that University'.[4] The Sheridan family were no strangers to Cork. His uncle, Thomas Sheridan (1661-1688), another brother of the Bishop of Kilmore, was one of the most fervent Jacobites of the time. He was appointed Collector of Customs in Cork. In 1687 James II appointed him Chief Secretary and Commissioner of the Revenue in Ireland, and after the defeat of the Jacobite cause, he accompanied James into exile. It follows, therefore, that, with the change of administration, the Sheridans were suspect as being unrepentant Jacobites. Professor Landa points out the many great difficulties, and the reasons attaching to them which prevented Swift from obtaining preferment for those whom he considered worthy – 'Since the Whigs remained in power during Swift's tenure as dean, he continued to be an irritated spectator of political intrigue and preferment as various members of his chapter ascended to the episcopal bench; and to the end he regularly complained that he could not get preferment for worthy clergymen among his canons because of party'.[5] When Carteret was appointed Lord Lieutenant, Swift used his influence with him, as an old friend, to secure the incumbency of Rincurran for Sheridan: 'I have only one humble Request to make your Excellency... and it is in favour of Mr. Sheridan. I beg you will take your Time for bestowing him some church-preferment to the value of £140 a year. He is agreed on all Hands to have done much publick Service by many Degrees in the Education of Youth than any five of his Vocation, and hath much more Learning than usually falls to the share of those who profess to teaching... His greatest Fault is a Wife and seven Children, for which there is no excuse but that a Wife is thought necessary to a Schoolmaster...'.[6]

Swift's plea was successful. When Carteret appointed Sheridan to Rincurran, Baron Pocklington wrote to Bishop Wake expressing surprise that Sheridan, 'second to Swift in the Battle about the halfpence'[7] had been given a living by Carteret. At that time, too, in addition to his strong opposition against the policy of the British government in filling Irish benefices with clergymen from England, instead of preferring those born and educated in Ireland,[8] Swift was concerned in defending right of property in tithes. Swift was not sure that the ebullient Sheridan could be relied upon to do all these things in his (Sheridan's) own interest which his duties and rights required. First he wrote Lord Carteret returning 'my most humble thanks for your favour to Mr. Sheridan'.[9] Then he wrote Sheridan – 'You are an unlucky devil, to get a living the furthest in the kingdom from Quilca'.[10] and added this advice as to how he was to act towards his Bishop: 'If you are under the Bishop of Cork, he is a capricious gentleman; but you must flatter him monstrously upon his learning and his writings, that you have read his book against Toland, a hundred times and his sermons (if he has printed any) have been always your model'.[11] At the same time, Swift sends Sheridan a letter 'inclosed to him, which I desire you will seal. Mrs Johnson puts me in mind to caution you not to drink or pledge any health in his Company for you know his weak side in the matter'.[12] Swift has fears or misgivings about Sheridan's tongue: 'Take the Oaths heartily to the Powers that be, and remember that Party was not made for depending Puppies'.[13] Elrington Ball reads this to mean that Swift suspected Sheridan to entertain Jacobite leanings.[14] Others held the same view, and it seems a reasonable probability that just as Swift was, at one time, under surveillance and suspicion, so also was Thomas Sheridan when in order to oblige Archdeacon Russell of Cork, he accepted an invitation from the Archdeacon to preach a sermon on that fateful August 1st. There are two accounts of this incident – one given by Sheridan's son, Thomas, in his *Life of Swift* is as follows:

'When he went down to be inducted into his living, he was requested by Archdeacon Russell[15] of Cork to supply his place in the pulpit on the following Sunday. The Doctor,who was a very absent man, had forgot his engagement, and was sitting quietly at his lodgings en deshabille when a message from the Parish Clerk, who saw no preacher arrive after the service had begun, roused him from his reverie. He dressed himself with all speed, and of two sermons that he had brought with him, took the first that came into his hand, without looking into it. It happened that the first of August in that very year fell on that very Sunday; and the first of August being the day on which Queen Anne died, was in that time of party, a day of great celebrity, and much adverted to by the Whigs. But this circumstance had not, at all, occurred to the Doctor, who looked on it, only as a common Sunday, without considering the day of the month. The text of this led-sermon happened to be 'Sufficient unto the Day is the evil thereof'. Such a text on such a day, excited a general murmur throughout the whole congregation, to the surprise of the Preacher, who was the only person ignorant of the cause: of which he was not informed till after he had descended from the pulpit, when the affair was past remedy. There happened to be present in the Church a furious Whig, and one of the most violent party men of the time. He, immediately, took post to Dublin, where by his representation of this matter... such a clamour was raised by the zeal of one man... the Lord Lieutenant... was obliged to order the Doctor's name to be struck out of the List of Chaplains...'.[16]

The second account is contained in a pamphlet published by Swift entitled *A Vindication of his Excellency the Lord C-t, from the charge of favouring none but the Tories, High Churchmen and Jacobites* (1730). In the course of this, Swift wrote:

'The first Person of a Tory Denomination, to whom his Excellency gave any Marks of his Favour, was Doctor Thomas Sheridan... The Doctor being well known, and distinguished for his Skill and Success in the Education of Youth, beyond most of his Profession for many Years past; was recommended to his Excellency on the score of his Learning, and particularly for his Knowledge in the Greek Tongue;... some time after he gave the Doctor a Churchliving, to the Value of almost one Hundred Pounds a Year, and made him one of his Chaplains; from an antiquated Nation, that good School-masters ought to be encouraged in every Notion, professing Civility and Religion. Yet his Excellency did not venture to make this bold Step, without strong recommendations from Persons of undoubted Principles, fitted to the Times; who thought themselves bound in Justice, Honour, and Gratitude, to do the Doctor a good Office, in return for the Care he had taken of their Children, or those of their Friends. Yet the Catastrophe was terrible: For the Doctor, in the Height of his Felicity and Gratitude, going down to take Possession of his Parish, and furnished with a few led-Sermons, whereof, as it is to be supposed, the Number was very small, having never served a Cure in the Church; he stopt at Cork, to attend on his Bishop; and going to Church on the Sunday following, was, according to the usual Civility of Country Clergymen, invited by the Minister of the Parish to supply the Pulpit. It happened to be the First of August; and the First of August happened that Year to light upon a Sunday: And it happened that the Doctor's Text was in these Words: sufficient unto the Day is the Evil thereof; and lastly, it happened that some one Person of the Congregation, whose Loyalty made him watchful upon every Appearance of Danger to his Majesty's Person and Government, when Service was over, gave the Alarm. Notice was immediately sent up to Town; and by the Zeal of one Man of no large Dimensions of Body or Mind, such a Clamour was raised, that we in Dublin could apprehend no less than an Invasion by the Pretender, who must be landed in the South. The Result was, that the Doctor must be struck out of the Chaplains List, and appear no more at the Castle'.[17]

The 'furious Whig… of no large Dimensions of Body or Mind' was one Richard Tighe,[18] of whom we shall have something to say. He is identified by a letter written by Dr. Coghill to the Rt. Hon. Edward Southwell. This letter is cited in the Council Book of Kinsale under date October 9th 1725 –

'My Lord-Lieut. gave the living of your town of Kinsale (Rincorran) to Mr. Sheridan, and he being at Cork, on 1 Aug. preached, and took for his text, 'Sufficient to the day is the evil thereof': this was, immediately, brought to town, and Mr. Tighe mentioned it to my Lo-Lieut, much to the prejudice of Sheridan, upon which he was forbid the Castle'.[19]

There are, we confess, a number of puzzling features regarding the incident which cannot, completely, be answered. First, was it coincidence or design that Sheridan was asked to preach on Aug. 1st in Archdeacon Russell's Church? The actual Church in which Sheridan preached was the oldest Church then standing in the City. This Church was taken down in 1782 and the present structure, which replaced it, is now closed to public worship. The congregation was likely to be among the most important in the City and, if Sheridan anticipated 'to supply the pulpit' on the invitation of the Minister of the Parish 'according to the usual civility of country clergymen', why should he have forgotten to attend a service on, of all days, Sunday? And, if the invitation to preach had come earlier that week, is it possible that Sheridan gave no thought, at all, to an occasion which was to be of such importance to him, to the extent that he was unprepared, and had haphazardly to pick one of two sermons which he had brought with him, or that he would ignore Swift's warning to exercise care, so much so that he had no regard to the context of that which he delivered. What he said has not come down to us. We would have given much to have sat with Richard Tighe in the congregation, that Sunday, as Sheridan ascended the pulpit and opened his remarks with the text 'Sufficient unto the day is the evil thereof'. The text, itself, is the last sentence of the last verse of

Chapter 6 of the Gospel of St. Matthew. Significantly enough, the first verse of the seventh chapter opens with the text 'Judge not, that ye be judged'. But, one man came to judge that day. Sheridan, we note, wanted to publish the sermon, but Swift stopped him with'… and would not dream of printing your sermon, which is a project abounding with objections unanswerable, and with which I can fill this letter'.[20] We must ask ourselves, too, what Richard Tighe was doing in the Congregation, that day? We find it possible to answer this by suggesting that he had, deliberately, come with the knowledge that Sheridan would preach, and with hope that Sheridan would deliver a Sermon which could be challenged, and with the determination to do as much harm to him if, by so doing, he could hurt and affront Swift; for both he and Swift were enemies. Apart from the fact that Tighe was a 'furious Whig' and Swift a Tory, they were not on speaking terms – 'Why, Tighe and I, when he comes, shall not take any notice of each other. I would not do it much in this town though we have not fallen out'.[21] And later – 'I met Tighe and your Smyth of Lovet's yesterday by the Exchange. Tighe and I took no notice of each other'.[22] And, later still – 'Dick Tighe and I meet and never stir our hats. I am resolved to mistake him for Witherington the nasty little lawyer that came up to me so sternly at the Castle the day I left Ireland'.[23] And this hurtful and libellous piece of gossip from Swift's pen speaks for itself: – 'Dick Tighe and his wife lodged over against us; and he has been seen out of our upper windows, beating her two or three times: they are both gone to Ireland but not together; and he solemnly vows not to live with her. Neighbours do not stick to say, that she has a tongue: in short I am told, she is the most urging provoking devil that ever was born; and he a hot whiffling puppy, very apt to resent'.[24] Is it any wonder, therefore, that apart from obvious political resentment, Tighe would take any opportunity to injure Swift or offend him, and whether by accident or design, his presence in St. Peter's Church was in hope that Sheridan's sermon was the opportunity he was waiting for?

It does seem that Carteret had little choice in dismissing Sheridan from his chaplaincy to the Lord Lieutenant. Carteret's own position was, as shown by the criticisms, somewhat suspect. Professor Landa suggests that 'Friendship between the Dean of St. Patricks and a Lord Lieutenant subject to Walpole may have done Carteret little good',[25] and he points to the fact that 'the Government, wary of Carteret for several reasons, limited his Church patronage at his second appointment as viceroy in 1727',[26] and

cites the observation of Bishop Goodwin that the men Carteret chose for
preferment never 'went under the denomination of Whiggs'.[27] When
Carteret dismissed Sheridan as one of his Chaplains, Swift wrote Sheridan
on Sept. 11th 1725 – 'If you are indeed a discarded Courtier, you have
reason to complain but none at all to wonder... It is safer for a man's
interest to blaspheme God, than to be of a party out of power, or even to
be thought so. And since the last was the case, how could you imagine that
all mouths would not be open when you were received and in some manner
prefer'd by the Government, tho' in a poor way? I tell you there is hardly
a Whig in Ireland who would allow a potatoe and Butter-milk to a reputed
Tory... Too much Advertency is not your Talent, or else you had fled
from that Text, as from a Rock. For as Don Quixote said to Sancho, what
business had you to speak of a Halter, in a Family where one of it was
hanged?'[28] Swift went on to rebuke Sheridan –'... It is indeed against
Common Sense to think that you should chuse such a Time, when you
had received a Favour from the Lord Lieutenant had had reason to expect
more, to discover your Disloyalty in the Pulpit. But will that avail?
Therefore sit down and be quiet, and mind your own Business as you
should do, and contract your Friendships, and expect no more from Man
than such an animal is capable of, and you will every day find my description of Yahoos more resembling'. Swift did not end his rebuke
without adding – '...you believe, every one will acquit you of any Regard
to temporal interest, and how came you to claim an Exception from all
mankind?... for being of a weak constitution, in an Employment pre-
carious and tiresome, loaden with children cum uxore neque lini neque
commoda, a man of intent and abstracted thinking, enslav'd by Mathe-
matics, and Complaint of the world, this new weight of Party malice hath
struck you down, like a Feather on a horses back, already loaden as far as
he is able to bear. You ought to change the Apostle's Expression, and say,
I will strive to learn in whatever state etc.'[29] Swift had no doubt, as he says,
that Sheridan was struck down by 'Party malice' and he resolved and set
out to deal with Tighe as he had dealt with Whitshed, and would deal with
Bettesworth, The Duchess of Somerset, the Legion Club and others, and
Tighe was to know and suffer the full force and effect of a Swift lampoon.[30]
Swift expresses his strong feeling of indignation in a letter which he wrote
on Sept. 18th, 1725, to Thomas Tickell, who had been under-Secretary to
Addison and who had, on June 6th 1724, been appointed Chief Secretary
of Ireland:

'Here is Mr. Sheridan perpetually teazing me with Complaints directly in the style I have often met among State Letters of Loss of Favour by misrepresentation and Envy and Malice, and secret Enemyes, and the rest of that Jargon... The worst evil is, that when ill opinions are instilled into great Men, they never think it worth their while to be undeceived, and so a little man is ruined without the least tincture of guilt... I was the person who recommended Mr. Sheridan... I do believe Mr. Sheridan hath been formerly reckoned Tory... And I hope a Man may be a convert without being a Renegade... It is most infallible by all sorts of Reasons that Mr. Sheridan is altogether innocent in that accusation of Preaching, but, as he is a creature without Cunning, so he hath not overmuch Advertency... But he hath other good Qualityes enough to make up that Defect, Truth, Cander, good Nature, pleasantness of Humor, and very good Learning, and it was upon these Regards I was bold to recommend him, because I thought it was for the general good that he should have some Encouragement to go on with his Drudgery. But if it be determined that Party must lay her Talons upon him, there is no more to be said... and yet it is hard that even a beggar should suffer who is wholly innocent... and if Mr. Sheridan guesses right of the person who is his Chief Accuser' (Swift obviously refers to Tighe) 'there is no Man who is not Altogether drunk and mad with Party would value the accusation.'[31]

Swift makes it clear that he has 'Title to your Favour' and pleads that – 'If by the Clutter made upon this occasion, it should be thought most proper for Mr. Sheridan not to appear about the Castle at this juncture, I believe he will content himself, but not that he should lose any Degree of Favor with his Excellency; and if this be the case, I hope you will so order, that My Lord will condescend to signify so much to Him – For I know too well how often Princes themselves are obliged to act against their judgment amidst the Rage of Factions'.[32] Before Swift sent this letter to Tickell, he asked Sheridan to read it – 'and if you do not dislike it, let it be sent'.[33] Swift wants to make certain that Tighe was Sheridan's accuser – '...are you certain of the accuser that it is Tighe?'[34] He promises that 'When I come to Town, I shall see the Lord Lieutenant and be as free with him as possible'.[35] He assured Sheridan that 'my Lord Lieutenant believes, no more your Guilt than I, and therefore it can be nothing but to satisfy the Noise of Party at this juncture, that he acts as he does; and if so (as I am confident it is) the effect will cease with the cause. But without doubt Tighe and others have dinned the words Tory and Jacobite into his Excellency's Ears, and therefore your Text, etc., was, only, made use of as an opportunity'.[36] One point must, here, be made clear. No attempt was made, nor could it, reasonably, in the circumstances have been made, to deprive Sheridan of his living of Rincurran. The penalty imposed upon him was to have his name removed from the Lord Lieutenant's list of Chaplains, and to lose, as Swift pointed out, the chance of further preferment. That this meant a considerable loss was recognised, and by none more, it is stated, than Archdeacon Russell, at whose invitation Sheridan had preached. It is stated that the Archdeacon was so distressed with the disaster which Sheridan had suffered and regarding himself 'however accidental' as responsible for the ruination of Sheridan's aspirations, and having no family of his own, but being a man of property, he most generously made over to Sheridan by Deed of Gift the Manor of Drumlane in Co.Cavan worth £250 a year. This statement, by Sheridan's son,[37] is apparently correct. Drumlane is a parish in the Barony of Lower Loughtree, County of Cavan, and Province of Ulster, on the road from Clones to Ballyconnell. There is one important peculiarity: One would have expected that a search in the Irish Registry of Deeds would have disclosed a memorial of the gift. With this view, we made a most careful and prolonged search, but it failed to disclose any dealings with lands in which Archdeacon Russell or Sheridan were both concerned. Nevertheless, Swift himself, implies that he had knowledge of the Archdeacon's generosity when he wrote Sheridan. 'Upon the whole matter you are no loser, but at least have got something'[38] and a letter from Sheridan to Swift, written on August 16th 1734 in that mock language in which they both loved to communicate, said – '...Eye a Mag owing two Bell turbet two meet they ten Ants off Drum lean too race heave mow knee butt Eye fare Ice hall me taw a par cell off M T Pock heats'.[39] Sir Harold Williams renders this as – 'I am a-going to Belturbet to meet the tenants of Drumlane to receive money, but I fear I shall meet a parcel of empty pockets'.[40] Also, Sheridan provides evidence that the Corkman's generosity was as great as has been claimed for him, for again, on December 25th 1734, he writes to Swift, as follows: 'Eye ray mice elf too May jor Par rots yes stair day morn in Two mete ten ants off Drum lean, two pea me sum Mow knee den off Michael Mass and March Gale. Eye sup hose Eye shall race heave a bout to hun dread pounds, or they raw bouts'[41] which Sir Harold Williams reads as

'I rid myself to Major Perrotts yesterday morning to meet the tenants of Drumlane to pay me some money due of Michaelmas and March gale. I suppose I shall receive about two hundred pounds, or thereabouts'.[42] Our search in the Registry of Deeds however disclosed a transaction between Swift and Sheridan, which took place on 13th March 1734, and in which Sheridan assigned to Swift – 'ye Pole of land of Blencoop als Blenamp in the Parish of Killmore, two poles of Church land Called Marrahill and Anagh and one pole of land called Drumcorr all being land held by Sheridan by virtue of a Lease from the Bishop of Millmore', and Sheridan who was perpetually in debt, acknowledged on July 5th 1735 that he had sold these lands to Swift.[43] It has already been made clear that Sheridan did not lose his incumbency of Rincurran. Indeed, he held this until 1730, when he exchanged it for the Vicarage of Dunboyne and Kilbride in Meath diocese. The latter preferment he exchanged also in 1734 for the Mastership of the Royal School at Cavan.

Swift promised Sheridan '...When my Lord is in London we may clear a Way to him to do you another Job, and you are young enough to wait'.[44] As to Tighe – 'I do think it is agreed that All animals fight with the Weapons natural to them (which is a new and wise Remark out of my own Head) and the Devil take that Animal, who will not offend his Enemy, when he is provoked, with his proper Weapon; and though your old dull Horse little values the Blows I give him with the Butt-end of my stick, yet I strike on and make him wince in Spight of his Dulness; and he shall not fail of them while I am here; and I hope you will do so too to the Beast who has kicked against you, and try how far his Insensibility will protect him, and you shall have Help, and he will be vexed, for so I found your Horse this day, though he would not move the faster. I will kill that flea or louse which bites me, though I get no Honour by it'.[45] That Sheridan was quite capable of lampoons and other satirical compositions is without doubt. In language as coarse as any which Swift could use, he writes of Tighe to Swift (the interpretation of the letter is supplied by Sir Walter Scott)[46] – 'I writ a Tory pamphlett', (was this a reference to the form and subject of his Cork sermon?) 'and Dick Tighe tore all, every bit. Dick is a beast. Dick is a serpent, I say, Dick is a turd, I say. Dick is a farter. Dick is pist, I say. Dick is a vixen. Dick is a squittering, nasty, fusty, musty cur. Dick is a ranter. Dick is a baboon, I say. Said I to Dick Tighe, can't you come in as a dancing master, and dance a bory or a minuet? Damme if I do, said Dick. K – my a –, said I, you puppy. You're a sturdy ruffian, said I.

You're a Tory villain, said Dick. You're fit for a gallows, said I, and you may die a-dancing. You're a rascally cur, said Dick. Dick Tighe, said I, your rage is a fart to me.

> 'Tantivy, said I, tantivy,
> Hy! for a Dick in a privy'.

'I made Dick as tame as a mouse for all his anger. I recollect a piper, said I, and a trumpeter, and a shoemaker, and a drummer, and a squire, and a blackamore in your Company, and a deal more making a jest o'you, Tighe. It is all a lie, a damme, said Dick, as sure as I stink. Since you say so, I say no more'.[47]

Swift appears to have waited until 1728 before publishing a satire in a newspaper called *The Intelligencer* which was written, jointly, with Sheridan. The satire was entitled '*Mad Mullinix and Timothy*'. The character Timothy clearly referred to Tighe –

> 'I own 'tis not my Bread and Butter,
> But Prithee Tim, why all this clutter?
> Why ever in these raging fits,
> Damning to Hell the Jacobits?
> When, if you search the Kingdom round,
> There's hardly twenty to be found'
>
> . . . .
>
> 'In every A – you run your Snout,
> To find this Damn Pretender out'.[48]

Swift followed up this attack, 'striking on' in more lurid language in *Tim and The Fables* in which he likened Tighe to 'the Monkey who had seen the world' comparing:

> 'His own sweet Figure with the Print,
> Distinguish'd ev'ry Feature in't;
> The Twist, the Squeeze, the Rump, the Fidge an'all
> Just as they lookt in the original',[49]

and concluded with:

'Dear Tim, no more such angry speeches,
Unbutton and let down your Breeches,
Tare out the Tale, and wipe your A –
I know you love to act a Farce'.[50]

Meanwhile, on Oct. 16th 1730, John Jephson succeeded Sheridan as Rector of Rincurran[51] while Sheridan returned to Schoolmastering and poverty.

Swift pays the greatest and most sincere tribute to Sheridan in writing – 'You were born to be happy, for you take the least piece of good Fortune cheerfully',[52] but it was the Earl of Cork who wrote this summation of his life and character –

'Dr. Sheridan was a school-master, and in many instances, perfectly well adapted for that station. He was deeply versed in the Greek and Roman languages; and in their customs and antiquities. He had that kind of good nature, which absence of mind, indolence of body, and carelessness of fortune produce; and although not over strict in his own conduct, yet he took care of the morality of his scholars, whom he sent to the University remarkably well founded in all classical learning, and not ill instructed in the social duties of life. He was slovenly, indigent and cheerful. He knew books better than men and he knew the value of money least of all… he remained a punster, a quibbler, a fiddler, and a wit. Not a day passed without a rebus, an anagram, or a madrigal. His pen and his fiddle stick were in continual motion; and yet to little or no purpose…'.[53]

Sheridan died on 10th Oct. 1738, shortly after a quarrel with Swift, arising from Sheridan's promise to bring any instances of Swift's well-known avarice to the Dean's attention. Orrery wrote Swift on Jan. 2nd, 1738/1739. Somehow, it seems to us that Orrery's words, written in his flamboyant, grandiloquent style, may well be adopted as Sheridan's own estimate of himself, and his friendship for Swift –

'The New Year begins as the old year ended, in Storms, in Rain and all the various Inclemencies of the Sky. The New Year finds me in the same situation the Old year left me, a domestic animal fond of my own Home, and loth to quit my Chimney Corner. Year may turn round after year still I must be your faithful servant. The Rage of Storms, the whistling of Winds, the Roar of Thunder, can make no impression upon my Breast, whatever effect they may have upon the politics and proceedings of the mighty and the great'.[54]

CHAPTER III

Notes

1. *Swift and the Church of Ireland*, Louis A. Landa, p. 87, hereafter cited as 'Landa'.
2. *Clerical and Parochial Records of Cork, Cloyne and Ross*, Vol. 1, p. 233, W. Maziere Brady D.D. (Alex. Thom, Dublin, 1863), hereafter cited as 'Brady'.
3. *Council Book of the Corporation of Kinsale,* ed. Richard Caulfield, p. cxxiv.
4. Brady, Vol. 1, p. 234.
5. Landa, p. 91.
6. Swift to Lord Carteret, 17th April 1725. Corr. (Williams), Vol. 3, p. 57/58.
7. Wake Correspondence (14th July 1725) cited by Landa, p. 175, n. 1.
8. Swift to Lord Carteret, July 3rd, 1725. Corr. (Williams), Vol. 3, p. 70.
9. Ibid.
10. Corr. (Williams), Vol. 3, p. 66.
11. Ibid.
12. Swift to Rev. Thomas Sheridan, 29th June 1725; Corr. (Williams) Vol. 3, p. 68.
13. Swift to Rev. Thomas Sheridan, June 28th, 1725: Corr. (Williams) Vol. 3, p. 67.
14. Note by Sir Harold Williams at Corr. Vol. 3, p. 67.
15. Thomas Russell was Archdeacon of Cork and Rector of Ardnegihy. He was the eldest son of Lieut. Col. John Russell, of Rutland, Co. Carlow, a kinsman of Peter Browne, Bishop of Cork; was born at Lisburn and entered Trinity College at the age of fourteen years as Pensioner. In 1725 he was made Vicar-General of Cork and Ross.
16. *Life of Swift*, by Thomas Sheridan, pp. 333-334.
17. Prose Works, Vol. 12, pp. 153-169, ed. Davis.
18. Richard Tighe was M.P. for Belturbet, a strong Whig and a person of influence in Ireland. It is significant, perhaps, that he had considerable support in Cork, of which city on May 13th 1730 he was made a freeman: that the right hon. Richard Tighe esq. be presented with his freedom in a silver box by the mayor, that Mr. Webber answered Mr. Tighe and thanked him for his care of the interests of the city, Caulfield, p. 491.
19. Council Book of the Corporation of Kinsale, p. cxxiv.
20. Swift to Sheridan, 11th Sept. 1725: Corr. (Williams), Vol. 3, p. 95.
21. *Journal to Stella*: Letter VII, Oct. 1710, Vol. 1, p. 71.
22. Ibid. Letter XXIII, Jan. 1710, Vol. 1, p. 158.
23. Ibid. Letter XXIII, May, 1711, Vol. 1, p. 268.
24. Ibid. Letter XXVII, Aug. 1711, Vol. 1, p. 343.
25. Landa, p. 174.

26. Ibid.
27. Ibid. pp. 174/175.
28. Corr. (Williams) Vol. 3, p. 93.
29. Ibid.
30. Swift sought revenge by lampooning Tighe in *Mad Mullinix and Timothy, The Legion Club*, and by attacking him in *Vindication of Lord Carteret*.
31. Corr. (Williams) Vol. 3, pp. 97/98.
32. Ibid. p. 98.
33. Swift to Sheridan: Corr. (Williams) Vol. 3, p. 99.
34. Ibid. p. 99.
35. Ibid.
36. Ibid. pp. 99/100.
37. *Life of Swift*: Thomas Sheridan, p. 383.
38. Corr. (Williams) Vol. 3, p. 100.
39. Corr. (Williams) Vol. 4, p. 246.
40. Ibid. n. 2.
41. Corr. (Williams) Vol. 4, p. 280.
42. Ibid. n. 4.
43. Ibid. p. 357.
44. Corr. (Williams), Vol. 3, p. 100.
45. Swift to Sheridan, Sept. 25th 1725: Corr. (Williams) Vol. 3, p. 101.
46. See Sir Harold Williams' note at Vol. 4, Corr. p. 363.
40. Ibid. p. 363.
48. Poems, Vol. 3, p. 773, ll. 1-6; 25-26.
49. Ibid. p. 783, ll. 15-18.
50. Ibid. ll. 35-38.
51. Brady, Vol. 1, p. 235.
52. Swift to Sheridan: Corr. (Williams) Vol. 4, p. 349.
53. Remarks, pp. 84-86.
54. *The Orrery Papers*, vol. 1, p. 248.

'Never man spake like this man'

How was a Bishop of Cork elected in the eighteenth century? 'An eighteenth-century clergyman often needed the temperament and skill of the politician to achieve success in Church affairs'.[1] Swift, who had achieved so much as a politician, was unable to advance his own ambitions:

> 'A place he got, yclyp'd a stall,
> And eke a Thousand pounds withall;
> And, were he a less witty Writer,
> He might, as well, have got a Mitre'.[2]

'We are told by everybody' writes Sir Constantine Phipps to Swift 'that the rest of our vacant Bishopricks will be fill'd to our satisfaction. If they are you must be one of them'. But, Swift knew that there were two great obstacles to his being preferred. The first was that he was an Irishman: 'Since your Excellency hath had an opportunity so early in your Government of gratifying your English Dependants by a Bishoprick and the best Deanery in the Kingdom, I cannot but hope that the Clergy of Ireland will have their Share in your Patronage. There is hardly a Gentleman in the Nation, who hath not a near Alliance with some of that Body; and most of them have Sons, usually breed one to the Church; although they have been of late years much discouraged and discontented, by seeing strangers to the country almost perpetually taken into the greatest Ecclesiastical Preferments, and too often, under Governors very different from your Excellency, the Choice of Persons was not to be accounted for either to Prudence or Justice'.[3] And Swift went on to say – 'The misfortune of having Bishops perpetually from England, as it must needs quench the Spirit of Emulation among us to excel in learning and the study of Divinity, so it produces another great discouragement... It will become so excellent a Governor as you, a little to moderate this great Partiality; wherein as you

St. Multose Church, Kinsale

will act with Justice and Reason, so you will gain the Thanks and Prayers of the whole Nation, and take away one great Cause of universal discontent: For I believe your Excellency will agree, that there is not another Kingdom in Europe where the Natives (even those descended from the Conquerors) have been treated as if they were almost unqualify'd for any Employment either in Church or State'.[4]

On 13th November 1709, Dive Downes, Bishop of Cork and Ross, suddenly died and on 11th January 1709/10 Peter Browne D.D. was appointed Bishop of Cork and Ross. Bishop Downes' illness was known to members of the clergy and, on the very day of his death, Swift was writing Lord Halifax soliciting his support in as wide terms as possible; thus – 'Yet all these are Trifles in comparison of having such a Solicitor as your Lordship of which I will make this use, that if you think this gentle Writer will not carry off Dr. South, or that his Reversion is not to be compassed your Lordship would please to use your Credit, that as My Lord Somers thought of me last year for the Bishoprick of Waterford, so my Lord President may now think on me, for that of Cork, if the Incumbent dyes of the Spotted Fever he is now under'.[5] Swift tells us that there was another candidate for the Bishoprick, one Dr. Lloyd 'Fellow of Dublin-College, noted in that Kingdom for being the only clergyman that declared for taking off the sacramental test'.[6] With a deliberate intent to wound, he describes how '...the doctor attended his Excellency to Ireland, and observing a cast wench in the family to be in much Confidence with my lady, he thought by addressing there, to have a short open Passage to Preferment. He met with great Success in his Amour, and walking one Day with his mistress after my Lord and Lady in the Castle Garden, my Lady said to his Excellency, 'What do you think? We are going to lose poor Foidy' (a Name of Fondness they usually gave her). 'How do you mean?' said my Lord; 'Why the doctor behind us is Resolved to take her from us'. 'Is he by G– ? Why, then, G–d d-mn me, he shall have the first bishoprick that falls. The Doctor thus encouraged, grew a most violent lover, returned with his Excellency for England, and soon after, the bishoprick of Cork falling void, to shew he meant fair, he married his damsel publicly here in London and his Excellency, as honourably engaged his Credit to get him the Bishoprick; but, the matter was reckoned so infamous, that both the Archbishops here, especially his Grace of York, interposed with the Queen to hinder so great a Scandal to the Church, and Dr. Browne, the Provost of Dublin College being then in town Her

Majesty was pleased to nominate him'.[7] Swift's bitter disappointment can be easily understood.

It is a pity, in a sense, that Cork was deprived of the honour of having Jonathan Swift as Bishop. It was not to be. Indeed, the hope that he might be translated to the Bishoprick of Cloyne, Co.Cork was disappointed when Henry Maule was appointed: 'As to what you say about Promotion you will find it was given immediately to Maule (as I am told) and I assure you that I had no offer, nor would accept them my behaviour to those in Power hath been directly contrary since I came here'.[8] And again, explaining his being passed over for Cloyne, he writes Rev. James Stopford – '...But all this made a great noise, and soon got to Ireland, from whence upon the late death of the Bishop of Cloyne, it was said I was offered to succeed, and I received many letters upon it, but there was nothing of truth for I was neither offered, nor would have received, except upon conditions which would never be granted. For I absolutely broke with the first Minister... I am, besides, all to pieces with the Lord-Lieutenant, whom I treated very roughly, and absolutely refused to dine with him',[9] and, with obvious bitterness, Swift adds – 'I think it would be better to live in England... you have the advantage to be a native of London; here you will be a freeman and in Ireland a slave. Here your competitors will be strangers, there every rascal your contemporary, will get over your head by the merit of party'.[10] Swift always insisted that he would not ask for any preferment for himself. He protests to Archbishop King on 1st Oct. 1711 – 'Perhaps in Ireland, I may not be able to prevent contempt any other way than by making my Fortune, but, then it is my Comfort, that contempt in Ireland will be no sort of Mortification to me. When I was last in Ireland, I was above half the Time retired to one scurvy Acre of Ground, and I always left it with Regret. I am as well received and known at Court, as perhaps any man ever was of my Level: I have formerly been the like. I left it then, and will perhaps leave it now (when they please to let me) without any concern, but what a few months will Remove. It is my Maxim to leave great ministers to do as they please; and, if I cannot distinguish myself enough by being useful in such a way, as becometh a Man of Conscience and Honour, I can do no more; for I never will solicit for myself, although I often do for others'.[11] Archbishop King had written Swift a somewhat clumsy letter on September 1st 1771 – '...I promised to say something as to your own affairs; and the first thing is, not to neglect yourself on this occasion, but to make use of the favour and interest you have at present to procure you some preferment that may be called a settlement. Years come on, and after a certain age, if a man be not in a station that may be a step to better, he seldom goes higher. It is with men as with beauties, if they pass the flower, they grow stale, and lie for ever neglected. I know you are not ambitious; but it is prudence, not ambition, to get into a station, that may make a man easy, and prevent contempt when he grows in years. You certainly may now have an opportunity to provide for yourself, and I entreat you not to neglect it'.[12] Swift's indignation is preserved in his letter of September 12th 1711 to Stella – 'Did I tell you of the Archbishop of Dublin's last letter? He had been saying in several of his former, that he would shortly write me something about myself, and it looked as if he intended something for me; at last out it comes... he advises me to strike in for some preferment now I have friends; and secondly, he advises me, since I have parts, and learning, and a happy pew, to think of some new subject in Divinity not handled by others, which I should manage better than anybody. A rare spark this, with a pox! but, I shall answer him as rarely... he should have invited me over, and given me some hopes or promises. But hang him'.[13]

Peter Browne was well known to Swift: 'Pray Sr' he writes Dean Stearne on April 17th 1710, 'favor me as far as to present my Duty to my Lord Bishop of Cork, and I wish he knew how concerned I was not to find him at home when I went to wait on him before I left the Town'.[14] Even though Browne was a friend of Stella, Swift did not, especially, care for him – 'I ...sate with Ld Tr... he gave me a Letter from an unknown Hand relating to Dr. Browne Bp of Cork, recommending him to a better Bishoprick as a Person who opposed Ld Wharton, and was made a Bp on that Account, celebrating him for a great Politician &c, in that all directly contrary to his Character; which I made bold to explain'.[15] It may be that Swift's indifference towards, and impatience with his clerical superior resulted in Browne being appointed to the See of Cork. Swift did not like Archbishop Marsh, who is said to have been instrumental in bringing Browne to the notice of Queen Anne. Brady says that 'Brown was an austere, retired and mortified man, but a Prelate of the first rank for learning among his Brethren, and was esteemed as the best Preacher of his age for the Gracefulness of his Manner, and a fine Elocution. He studied and was Master of most exact and just Pronunciation heightened by the sweetest and most solemn Tone of voice, and set off by a serious air, and a venerable Person: all which united commanded the most awful attention in his hearers of all sorts'.[16] Dr. Charles Webster says that Archbishop Marsh is credited with using his influence in favour of Dr. Browne. He refers to Provost Hutchinson's manuscript essay on the College as ascribing Browne's appointment to a sermon preached before Queen Anne on the text, 'Never man spake like this man'. 'The state of the Church in the diocese was anything but satisfactory at the opening of the eighteenth century... Then, there was gross ignorance in England of Irish affairs. The Church was being used for political purposes, and in the bestowal of patronage political motives had almost a complete monopoly'.[17] The Primate, Archbishop Boulter, was concerned with advancing English interests and the filling of every important benefice in the country with Englishmen was almost an obsession with him. He is described as lacking 'in any of those sentiments on behalf of Ireland as Ireland which so stirred King, and which Swift so trenchantly gave expression to at all time'.[18]

It was the publication of Toland's *Christianity not Mysterious* which attracted Narcissus Marsh, who was then Archbishop of Dublin, to the cause of Peter Browne. Browne had asked the Archbishop for a loan of the book, and when sending it to him, Marsh requested that Browne should let him have his thoughts about it. Fortified by Marsh's own views, Browne put his answer to Toland's book in the form of a letter to Marsh, which was published in 1697 with the Archbishop's imprimatur. In 1699, the Provostship of Trinity College, Dublin, fell vacant, and Browne was appointed. Swift regarded Browne as a 'capricious Gentleman'[19] and gave Sheridan the warning and advice to which we have already referred in Chapter Three of this work. Whilst Browne devoted himself to advancing and improving his diocese, he was not as popular as he deserved. He was suspected of entertaining Jacobite sympathies when, on 4th November 1713, he delivered a charge to the clergy of the diocese which was later published under the title of *Drinking in Remembrance of the Dead*. The opinion adopted by the Bishop was that to drink to the memory of the dead is an abuse and profanation of the Lord's Supper, and the charge was manifestly directed against those friends of the Revolution who drank to the glorious, pious and immortal memory of King William. The question was not, as the Bishop said, whether we may have an honourable remembrance of great and worthy persons, nor whether we were to be well affected to the late Revolution, nor whether we ought to honour the memory of King William, nor whether we may remember an absent friend or our Sovereign by wishing them health and prosperity. There was no doubt in the Bishop's mind as to these matters, but, he said 'there is an application made of the action of drinking to a mere man, in that very manner which ought never be applied but to the Person of Christ'. The only, or chief, effect of the Bishop's charge was to provoke the drinkers of the toast to append to it the words 'in spite of' or 'and a fig for the Bishop of Cork'.[20] Browne died at Cork on 25th August 1735. News of his death was not long in reaching Swift. Once again, he does not lose the opportunity, in spite of his dignified protest to Archbishop King, to express his own hopes. He writes to Alexander Pope on Sept. 3rd 1735 and says:

'We have a Bishop dead Dr. Bram of Cork, the most speculative writer of his Age, and as Scholars tell me, excellent in his way, but, I never read much of his works. I hope the D of D now the Parlm[t] here is to meet will find a successor for once among the Whig Divines here, and yet those they named for Candidates are the very worst they could pick up. This Kingdom is now absolutely starving; by the means of every oppression that can possibly be inflicted on mankind – shall I not visit for these things sayth the Ld. You advise me right, not to trouble about the world. But oppressions torture me, and I cannot live without meat and drink, nor yet without money; and Money is not to be had, except they will make me a Bishop...'[21]

Froude suggests that in or about November 1713 Swift might have exchanged St. Patricks, to which he had just been promoted, for an Irish Bishoprick.[22] For this statement he relied upon a, then, unpublished letter from an Irish Judge, Mr. Justice Nutley, to Swift. This letter, dated 5th November 1713, is now available. It refers to the death of the Primate Archbishop Narcissus Marsh, and hints that 'the Deanery of St. Patricks is a fine preferment for a Lord Lieutenants Chaplain to jump into after one or two months service, and if you can be temped to part wth y[or] fine house in Dublin for an ill contrived one on a Country Bishoprick, I can easily cut out a scheme for the advancing some eminent worthy active Prelate to the Primacy, and so three good persons may be promoted at once'.[23] Swift appears to have taken seriously to the suggestion, and to have written Primate Lindsay, Marsh's successor, who replied on January 5th 1713 (-14) – 'Yours I received... and immediately got Mr. Justice Nutley to write to the Bishop of Killala... to know of him whither if we could get him translated to the Bishoprick of Raphoe, he would accept it:

And this day we received his answer that it was not worth his while... for so little advantage as that Bishoprick would bring him...'.[24]

On Browne's death Swift was to suffer further disappointment, for Robert Clayton was translated from the Bishoprick of Killala to that of Cork and Ross. Clayton was an Englishman from Preston, who had married Katherine, daughter of Lord Chief Baron Donnellan. He was a man of considerable wealth. He was also a man of considerable charm, as witness Dr. Ed. Barry who, writing to Swift's friend the Earl of Orrery on July 5th 1736, says:

'The Bishop of Corke never sees me but he asks when I heard from Lord Orrery, and expresses the warmest regard for yr Ldsp. He is resolved, I find, to make himself usefull and popular. He has twice preached and twice been at the Water Club. He has din'd with half the town, and half the town has din'd with him. He is a good, natural and agreeable man, and will make an excellent Bishop in this place'.[25]

The reference to the Water Club is to the Cork Harbour Water Club (now the Royal Cork Yacht Club) which was founded in 1720 and thus became the first established Yacht Club in the world.

Bishop Clayton was a man of whom Orrery could write to Thomas Southerne from Cork on March 20th 1736-37:

'We are not entirely void of elegance at Corke. We have a Bishop who, as He has travel'd beyond the Alps, has brought home with him, to the amazement of our merchantile Fraternity, the Arts and Sciences that are the ornament of Italy and the Admiration of the European world. He eats, drinks and sleeps in taste. He has pictures by Carlo, Morat, Music by Corelli, Castles in Air by Vitruvius; and on High-days and Holidays we have the Honour of catching Cold at a Venetian door... Are not We a happy People who can receive Blessings from heaven and from earth by the Breath of one and the same Plan? How different are our times to what they were? Under the Reign of Doctor Browne, our late Pastor, we trembled at a Bumper, and loath'd the glorious Memory. We were as silent and melancholy as Captives and we were strangers to mirth even by Analogy. Under the Reign of Dr. Clayton we sing Catches, read Pastor Fido, and talk Love. Thus if one Road does not lead to Paradise, we try another, and shall either get there by Analogy or by Taste at last'.[26]

In or about 1730, probably after he had been appointed to the See of Killala, he was building his Dublin town house, now No. 80 St. Stephens Green, with Richard Cassel as his Architect, a house decorated in the new rococo taste 'furnished' as Delaney wrote 'with vertues and busts and pictures that the Bishop brought with him from Italy'.[27] Orrery lost no time in congratulating Bishop Clayton 'upon your new House in Stevens Green... Mr. Percival was so kind as to go with me yesterday... I ventured no further than the Hall Door, from whence my Prospect was much confin'd, except when I look'd upwards to the sky. Your Palace, my Lord, appears finely upon Paper, and to shew you that the whole pleases me, I even admire your Coal Cellars. Your great Room will probably bring the Earl of Burlington over to this Kingdom...'.[28] No. 80 St. Stephen's Green now forms part of the eastern half of Iveagh House, Dublin, which was presented by Lord Iveagh to the Irish Government some years ago, and where many important State functions and receptions are, from time to time, held. Orrery, notwithstanding his encomiums of Bishop Clayton, was not above criticism of him. 'The Corke Court may possibly prove an Ignis fatuus: which to our knowledge will do as much mischeif as the worst blazing Star that ever Whiston dreamt of...'.[29]

Swift's failure to win preferment was attributed by him to the opposition of the Archbishop of York, Dr. John Sharp, and to the hatred which the Duchess of Somerset had for him. It is noteworthy that in August 1711, when Oxford and St. John talked about Swift to Queen Anne she said 'she had never heard of him'.[30] The Archbishop made it clear to the Queen, following upon the publication of *A Tale of a Tub*, that in his opinion the author, Swift, was unfit for a seat on the episcopal bench. The Duchess was enraged by the *Windsor Prophecy*.[31] The Duchess was Queen Anne's Mistress of the Robes, and because of her Whig loyalties, Swift and his friends wished to have her removed from office. Mrs Hasham, formerly Abigail Hill, a close friend of Swift, asked him not to publish it because, as proved right, she feared it would anger the Queen. It was, however, published. When Swift wrote *The Author Upon Himself*[32] he attributed his failure to obtain preferment to:

'... an – – – pursu'd,
A crazy Prelate, and a Royal Prude,
By dull Divines, who look with envious Eyes,
On ev'ry Genius that attempts to rise'.[33]

In the *Windsor Prophecy* Swift, referring to the Duchess of Somerset who had red hair and was married to a man named Thynne, wrote:

> 'And dear England, if ought I understond
> Beware of Carrots from Northumberland
> Carrots sown Thyn a deep root may get,
> If so be they are in Sommer set
> Their Conyngs mark thou, for I have been told,
> They Assassine when young and Poison when old.
> Root out these Carrots, O Thou, whose Name,
> Is backwards and forwards always the same;
> And keep close to Thee always that Name
> Which backwards and forwards is allmost the same.
> And England wouldst thou be happy still
> Bury those Carrots under a Hill'.[34]

Swift, unfortunately for himself, could not preach the right sermons. What might have happened if he had been appointed to the See of Cork cannot be anticipated. When one considers his opinion of Cork merchants, it is possible that there would have been a series of explosive outbursts. It is interesting to note, however, from the Orrery papers the high reputation which he had as a writer and politician in the City of Cork, and it falls to the lot of a Corkman. Dr. Edward Barry, to make this prophetic assessment of his position in the centuries to come:

> 'I'm concerned to hear that Swift is confin'd by some Disorder; I hope nothing but a bilious cholic, which a few Satyrical evacuations will remove. Horace was in every respect in his case, and with as little reason blam'd when he marked out some particular Persons, however he was determined to write on. The World has been always the same, but many centuries will scarce produce another Horace or Swift'.[35]

Froude provides what perhaps is the fairest summation of Swift's approach to preferment –

> 'At that still far distant period when religious and political passion will allow a hearing to historical truth, the merits of the small section of resident Anglo-Irish gentlemen who, under their heavy disadvantages,

refused to despair of their country will not fail of honourable recognition
…In the first rank of this honourable body stood Swift, the Dean of
St. Patricks. It could hardly be said of Swift that he had chosen to remain
in Ireland, for he too, had the chance been allowed him, would have
preferred an English rectory to the metropolitan Cathedral of the
miserable land of his birth. But, as fate had cast him there, and disdaining
the tricks by which he might have flattered his way, even under Walpole
and the House of Hanover, into the highest places in the Church, he
became, in the best and noblest sense, an Irish patriot'.[36]

With knowledge of Swift's ambitions and insight into his disappointments,
frustrations, failure to secure preferment and despair, we may approach
that most fierce epitaph which he composed for himself:

> Hic depositum est Corpus
> Ionathan Swift S.T.D.
> Hujus Ecclesiae Cathedralis
> Decani
> Ubi Saeva Indignatio
> Ulterius
> Cor lacerare nequit.
> Abi viator,
> Et imitare, si poteris,
> Strenuum pro virili
> Libertatis vindicatorem

(Here lies Jonathan Swift, Doctor of Sacred Theology, Dean of this
Cathedral, where the heart can no longer be lacerated by savage indignation. Go from here, traveller, and imitate, if you are able, one who
strenuously, and to the utmost, vindicated liberty).

Notes

1. This view represents not only that of the source from which it is taken. but, also, of almost all contemporary writers.
2. Landa, p. xiv citing (Smedley) Gulliveriana, p. 109.
3. Swift to Lord Carteret, July 3rd 1725. Corr. (Williams) Vol. 3, p. 70.
4. Ibid. pp. 70/71.
5. Swift to Lord Halifax, 13th Nov. 1709. Corr. (Williams) Vol. 1, p. 159.
6. *A Short Character of His Excellency Thomas Earl of Wharton, Lord Lieutenant of Ireland* – Prose Works, Vol. 3, p. 182, ed. Herbert Davis (Basil Blackwell, Oxford) 1957 '... But when he comes to deal with the Earl of Wharton, it must be admitted that he moved from examination to invective...' (Davis, p. xviii).
7. Ibid. pp. 182/183.
8. Swift to Rev. John Worrall, July 15th 1726: Corr. (Williams) Vol. 3, p. 142.
9. Swift to Rev. James Stopford, 20th July 1726: Corr. (Williams) Vol. 3, p. 144.
10. Ibid. p. 146.
11. Swift to Archbishop King, 1st Oct. 1711. Corr. (Williams) Vol. 1, p. 262.
12. Archbishop King to Swift, Sept 1st 1711. Ibid. p. 254.
13. *Journal to Stella*: Letter XXX, Vol. 1, pp. 358/359.
14. Swift to Dean Stearne, Ap. 17th 1710: Corr. (Williams) Vol. 1, pp. 162/163.
15. Journal: Letter LXVIII, p. 596.
16. Brady, Vol. 3, p. 69.
17. *The Diocese of Cork*, p. 320, citing Harris-Ware ii: *Writers of Ireland*, p. 296 (Guy & Co. Ltd. Cork, 1920).
18. Ibid. p. 303.
19. Swift to Sheridan, 28th June 1725: Corr. (Williams) Vol. 3, p. 66, op. cit., ch. 3 of this work.
20. J.C.A.H.S. Vol. 9, p. 279.
21. Swift to Alexander Pope: Corr. (Williams), Vol. 4, p. 385.
22. *The English in Ireland* Vol. 1, pp. 352-353 (Longmans, Green & Co. 1872).
23. Mr. Justice Nutley to Swift, 5th Nov. 1713. Corr. (Williams) Vol. 1, p. 402.
24. Primate Lindsay to Swift, Jan. 5th 1713-14: Corr. (Williams) Vol. 2, p. 1.
25. *The Orrery Papers*, Vol. 1. p. 168.
26. Ibid. pp. 206/207.
26. *Autobiography and Correspondence of Mary Granville, Mrs Delaney*, ed. by Lady Llanover and cited in *Records of the Georgian Society Dublin*, Vol. 2 (1910).
28. *The Orrery Papers*, Vol. 1, p. 177.
29. Ibid. p. 180.

30. *Life and Friendships of Dean Swift* by Stephen Gwynn, p. 149 (Thornton Butterworth Ltd, 1933).
31. Poems, Vol. I, p. 145.
32. Ibid. p. 193.
33. Ibid. ll. 1-4.
34. Ibid. p. 148.
35. Dr. Ed. Barry to Lord Orrery, Ap. 11th 1736, *The Orrery Papers*, Vol. 1, p. 156.
36. *The English in Ireland*, (Froude), Vol. 1, pp. 499-500.

CHAPTER FIVE

'A blast from the proper trumpet'

Jonah Barrington[1] reminds that in the early part of his life, the Irish press, though supposed to be under due restraint, was in fact quite uncontrolled. 'From the time of Dean Swift, and Drapier Letters, its freedom had increased at intervals not only as to public but private subjects'. We, accustomed to Courts adjudicating in litigation involving libel or slander, the award of heavy damages, the use of Injunction to restrain publication of matters of questionable taste, the availability of the judicial processes of discovery and interrogatories to secure information, may well marvel at the license afforded to 17th and 18th Century writers, and their apparent immunity from Judicial process. Alexander Pope could write of Lady Mary Wortley Montagu.

> 'From furious Sappho scarce a milder fate,
> P-x'd by her love, or libell'd by her hate'[2]

and she, or some other person, in reply could charge –

> 'But, as thou hat'st, be hated by mankind,
> And with the emblem of thy crooked mind
> Marked on thy back, like Cain, by God's own hand,
> Wander, like him, accursed through the land'[3]

without any recourse to the Courts for redress. Whatever about England, in Ireland 'the Judges were then dependent... but another reason, more extensively operating was that in those days, men who were libelled generally took the law into their own hands, and eased the King's Bench of great trouble by the substitution of a small sword for a Declaration, or a case of pistols for a Judgment; and these same articles certainly formed a greater check upon the propagation of libels than the twelve judges and thirty-six jurors, altogether, at the present day; and gave rise to a code of laws very different from what we call municipal'.[4] We think it singular that the greatest hater of his time, as was Swift, should offer the greatest condemnation of 18th Century man's inhumanity to man – 'We have just enough Religion to make us hate, but not enough to make us love one another'.[5] Swift left no doubt as to where he stood – '...the chief end I propose to myself in all my labors is to vex the world rather than divert it',[6] and 'When you think of the world, give it one lash more at my Request. I have ever hated all Nations, professions and communityes and all my love is towards individuals... but principally I hate and detest that animal called man'.[7] And, as a reason for this, he explains –

> 'For Gulliver divinely shews
> That humankind are all Yahoos'[8]

and while he conceded –

> 'Perhaps I may allow, the Dean
> Had too much Satyr in his vein
> And seem'd determin'd not to starve it
> Because no Age could more deserve it'[9]

he was aware that he could

> 'Safely write a smart Lampoon
> To expose the brisk Baboon'.[10]

Indeed, with that coarseness which characterised so much of his poetry, Swift sought nothing better than –

> 'Let me, tho' the Smell be Noisom,
> Strip their Bums; Let Caleb hoyse'em
> Then apply Alecto's Whip,
> Till they wriggle, howl and skip'.[11]

The case of Lord Chief Justice Whitshed is a classic example and forerunner of the ordeal of Richard Bettesworth, who was to play so important a part in Swift's life. When Swift published a pamphlet, *A Proposal for the*

Universal Use of Irish Manufacture[12] Whitshed was directed to prosecute the Printer 'with the utmost rigour of law'.[13] The Chief Justice had 'so quick an understanding, that he resolved, if possible, to out-do his orders... The Printer was seized and forced to give great bail. After his Tryal, the Jury brought him in 'Not Guilty'... The Chief Justice sent them back nine times, and kept them eleven hours, until being perfectly tired out, they were forced to leave the matter to the mercy of the Judge, by what they call a Special Verdict... But the cause being so very odious and impopular, the trial and the Verdict was deferred from one Term to another, until upon the Duke of G-ft-n, the Lord Lieutenant's arrival, his Grace after mature advice, and permission from England, was pleased to grant a noli prosequi'.[14] Swift seized upon Whitshed's motto on his coach – Libertas et Natale solum (Liberty and my native country) and in a lampoon written in the year 1724 scarified the Chief Justice with –

> 'Libertas et Natale Solum,
> Fine words, I wonder where you stol'um.
> Could nothing but thy chief Reproach
> Serve for a Motto on thy coach?'[15]

Not content with this, he savagely raked up Whitshed's family background, and noting that Alderman Mark Quin, Whitshed's maternal grandfather had cut his throat in 1724, wrote –

> 'The Church I hate, and have good Reason
> For there my Grandsire cut his Weazon:
> He cut his Weazon at the altar;
> I keep my Gullet for the Halter',[16]

and again –

> 'In Church your Grand-sire cut his Throat,
> To do the jobb too long he tarry'd
> He should have had my hearty Vote,
> To cut his Throat before he marry'd'.[17]

Not even death deterred Swift from attacking Whitshed's memory, for when the Chief Justice died, Swift wrote: – 'It is too well known that we are forced to obey some laws we never consented to; which is a condition I must not call by its true uncontroverted Name, for fear of Lord Chief Justice Whitshed's Ghost, with his Libertas et Natale solum, written as a motto on his Coach, as it stood at the door of the Court, while he was perjuring himself to betray both';[18] and when a murmur of protest was made against this indelicate piece of bad taste, Swift replied – 'Laying it therefore down for a Postulatum, which I suppose will be universally granted; That no little Creature of so mean a Birth and Genius had ever the Honour to be a greater Enemy to his Country, and to all kinds of virtue than He, I answer thus: Whether there be two different Goddesses called Fame, as some authors contend, or only one Goddess, sounding two different Trumpets, it is certain, that People distinguished for their Villainy, have as good a Title for a Blast from the proper Trumpet, as those who are most renowned for their Virtues, have for the other, and have equal reason to complain, if it be refused them...'.[19]

In much the same vein, Swift had lampooned William Wood, a merchant who had obtained Letters Patent authorising him to mint copper coinage for Ireland to the detriment of the nation. Swift pursued Wood in prose and verse. Thus:

> 'When Foes are o'ercome, we preserve them from Slaughter,
> To be Hewers of Wood, and Drawers of Water,
> Now, although to Draw Water is not very good,
> Yet we all should Rejoyce to be Hewers of Wood'.[20]

And again, not particular about his choice of words, he cuts and sneers with –

> 'I hear among scholars there is a great doubt,
> From what kind of Tree this Wood was hewn out,
> Teague made a good pun by a Brogue in his Speech,
> And said, By my Shoul he's the son of a Beech'.[21]

It is not to be wondered if we can find no pre-expressed desire on the part of Richard Bettesworth to dispute with the greatest satirist of all time. Bettesworth had no unusual distinctions. He was born in London, the son of a member of a well-known County Cork family, the Bettesworths of Mallow, who were among the earliest settlers in Mallow after the Desmond forfeiture, when the Jephson family became possessed of the Manor. Bettesworth, who had taken up residence in Dublin, was M.P. for Midleton County Cork from 1727 until his death in 1741. He was admitted to the Irish Bar in 1716, and in 1725 was awarded the degree of LL.D. (honoris causa) by Trinity College, Dublin. He practised as a Barrister on what is known as the Munster Circuit, and frequently appeared at the Cork Assizes. He was created Serjeant-at-Law in 1723.[22] On all sides, according to Dr. Elrington Ball, he appears to have been regarded as a 'blatant, pompous and self-sufficient individual'.[23] An anonymous Corkman using the pseudonym 'Pickle Herring'[24] sneered at him thus – 'Is it not sufficient for them to see a man of learning and law, a man of singular inimitable eloquence, a man of unparalleled graceful action, a man of unspeakable, inconceivable truth, justice and sincerity, exemplary religion, strict virtue, nice honour and sterling worth in general past finding out?'[25] Bettesworth was a member of the Landlord Class, which class Swift never ceased to criticise – 'I would now expostulate a little with our Country Landlords, who by unmeasurable screwing and racking their Tenants all over the Kingdom have, already, reduced the miserable people to a worse condition than the peasants in France...'.[26] More than this, Swift was, deeply and sincerely, concerned with what he considered to be the serious and worsening condition of the Irish Clergy; and the impending clash between Landlords and Clergymen as to the right of the Clergy to collect Tithe rents out of the rents earned from agistments. As to the first... 'It was pleasant to observe these Gentlemen, labouring with all their might, for preventing the Bishops from letting their Revenues at a moderate half Value (whereby the whole Order would, in an Age, have been reduced to manifest Beggary) at the very Instant when they were everywhere canting their own Lands upon short Leases, and sacrificing their oldest Tenants for a penny an acre advance'.[27] As to the second, it was clear that anyone who attempted to make further inroads on the right of the clergy to collect Tithes would unleash Swift's anger, and unite the Irish Bench of Bishops in firm resistance. When 'an Act for the Preservation of the Inheritances, Rights and Profits of Lands belonging to the Church and Persons Eccle-siastical'[28] was introduced into Parliament 'the Episcopal bench was aroused... and... the Bishops... were agreed that vigorous action was necessary'.[29] In a tract, published anonymously, and entitled *Some Arguments Against Enlarging the Power of Bishops, etc.*,[30] Swift, arguing that justice be equally applied to the clergy as well as to the people, said '...it

Bell Tower, Inniscarra

would be hard, if Ecclesiastical bodies should be the only Persons excluded from any Share in publick Advantages; which yet can never happen, without a greater Share of Profit to their Tenants. If God sends rain equally upon the Just and the Unjust, why should those who wait at his Altars, and are instructers of the People, be cut off from partaking in the general Benefit of Law, or of nature?'[31] Swift was prepared, too, to attack the Bench of Bishops, as he did in 1732, when he expressed the opinion that the Bishops were attempting to destroy the Church. In prose, he published anonymously a pamphlet entitled *On the Bill for the Clergy's Residing on their Livings and Considerations upon Two Bills*.[32] In a bitter lampoon he wrote –

> 'When CHRIST was betray'd to Pilate, the Praetor,
> In a dozen apostles but one prov'd a Traytor!
> One Traytor alone, and faithful Eleven;
> But we can afford you six Traytors in seven',[33]

and he charged –

> 'Our B–s pust up with Wealth and with Pride
> To Hell on the backs of the Clergy wou'd ride'.[34]

Whilst Swift had good reason to be grateful to the Irish House of Commons, as he acknowledged, he had good grounds, nevertheless, to anticipate further attempts to reduce the privileges of clergy. So it was that on 12th December 1733, what was to prove a fateful Bill for Richard Bettesworth was introduced into the House. It was entitled *Heads of a Bill for the Further Regulation and Improvement of the Flaxen and Hempen Manufacture*.[35] Bettesworth's name was not associated with it, as it was when, according to Order, on December 16th 1725, he presented to the House *Heads of a Bill for the Better Maintenance of Curates within the Church of Ireland*.[36] Indeed, the record shows that Messrs Hill, Lucas and Dobbs were ordered to 'prepare and bring in the same'. The purpose of the Bill was to lend aid to the linen industry, by reducing tithes on hemp and flax to a figure of one-third of the legal rate prevailing. Swift, on being appealed to by members of the Clergy, wrote a tract entitled *Some Reasons against the Bill for Settling the Tithe of Hemp, Flax etc. by a Modus*[37] and, in addition, he organised a Petition 'In Behalf of Themselves and the Rest of the Clergy of the Church of Ireland, as by Law Established, setting forth That they will be greatly affected in their properties by a clause in Heads of a Bill now before this House... and praying to be heard by their Counsel against the said clause'.[38] On Saturday, 29th December 1733, the Petitioners, by their Counsel, made their submissions and, as a result, certain changes were made in the Bill which the clergy, even if not entirely satisfied, regarded as reasonable. We do not know, exactly, what part Bettesworth took in the debate.[39] Sir Harold Williams suggests that 'Bettesworth strongly supported the Bill'.[40] Dr. Elrington Ball suggests that Bettesworth opposed the Petition which Swift and his friends had presented to the House through their Counsel, and attempted to controvert the arguments of Counsel'.[41] We know that it was, then, customary for Petitioners to attend with their Counsel in the House to listen to the arguments which were being presented on their behalf. It is more than likely, therefore, that Swift and his friends were witnesses, on the occasion, to Bettesworth's objections. Be this as it may, and whatever the nature of Bettesworth's objections may have been, we agree with Professor Landa, who notes that 'Swift's indignation was out of all proportion to the threat posed by the legislation'.[42] Within a short while, Swift and his friends had moved in to attack and devour the good name, reputation and career of Bettesworth. It was as if a wolf pack had fastened itself upon a victim, intent upon pursuing him to destruction. Not only Swift, but Rev. William Dunkin 'and the wits joined in the hue and cry',[43] and made Bettesworth's life a misery and a hell. It is said that Bettesworth's practice dwindled, and his health, which does not seem to have been good,[44] suffered to such an extent as to bring about his early death. We shall see, however, how Bettesworth, in what undoubtedly was an un-equal contest, reacted and fought back, and if our view of subsequent events in Cork are correct, in the end, secured some satisfaction for his sufferings. First, let us examine Swift's opening attack, and its consequences. In the *Gentleman's Magazine* Supplement 1733 was printed – 'On the Words – Brother Protestants, and Fellow Christians, so familiarly used by the Advocates for the Repeal of the Test Act in Ireland 1733',[45] in which –

'A Ball of new-dropt Horse's Dung,
Mingling with Apples in the Throng,
Said to the Pippin, plump and prim,
See, Brothers, how we Apples swim'[46]

and continued –

> 'Thus at the Bar that Booby Bettesworth,
> Tho' Half a Crown o'er pays his Sweat's Worth;
> Who knows in Law, nor Text, nor Margent,
> Calls Singleton his Brother Serjeant'.[47]

Swift denied that neither in doctrine or discipline were these men Brethren –

> 'But in no other Sense, than Nature
> Has made a Rat our Fellow Creature,
> Lice from your Body suck their Food;
> But is a Louse your Flesh and Blood?'[48]

It would be an understatement to say that Bettesworth was greatly incensed and allowed his passion to override that discretion which, normally is associated with the practice of law. We have two accounts of what followed, that of Sheridan,[49] who alleges that Bettesworth, armed with a penknife, went to the Deanery vowing to slice off Swift's ears. Swift was visiting with his Vicar, John Worral, whereupon Bettesworth went to Worral's house, and there, upon being confronted with the Dean, lost his nerve and withdrew. The second is contained in a long letter, carefully written and, to some extent, in self-adulatory terms, by Swift to the Duke of Dorset[50] –

'On Monday last week, toward evening, there came to the Deanry one Mr. Bettesworth; who, being told by the servants that I was gone to a friend's house, went thither to enquire for me, and was admitted into the street-parlour. I left my company in the backroom, and went to him. He began with asking me, whether I were the author of certain verses, wherein he was reflected on. The singularity of the man in his countenance, manner, action, style and tone of voice, made me call to mind that I had once seen him, about two or three years ago at Mr. Ludlow's country-house.[51] But I could not recollect his name, and of what calling he might be I had never heard. I therefore desired to know who, and what he was; said I had heard of some such verses, but knew no more. He then signified to me, that he was a serjeant-at-law, and a member of Parliament. After which, he repeated the lines that concerned him with great emphasis; said, I was mistaken in one thing, for he assured me he was no booby, but owned himself to be a coxcomb. However, that being a point of controversy wherein I had no concern, I let it drop. As to the verses, he insisted, that by his taste, and skill in poetry, he was as sure I writ them as if he had seen them fall from my pen. But I found the chief weight of his argument lay upon two words that rhymed to his name, which he knew could come from none but me. He then told me, That since I would not own the verses, and that since he could not get satisfaction by any course of law, he would get it by his pen, and shew the world what a man I was. When he began to grow over-warm and eloquent, I called in the gentleman of the house, from the room adjoining; and the Serjeant, going on with less turbulence, went away. He had a footman in the hall during all his talk, who was to have opened the door for one or more fellows, as he had since reported; and, likewise, that he had a sharp knife in his pocket, ready to stab or maim me. But the Master and Mistress of the house, who knew his character, and could hear every word from the room they were in, had prepared a sufficient defence in such a case, as they afterwards told me. He hath since related, to five hundred persons of all ranks, above five hundred falsehoods of this conversation, of my fears and his own brutalities, against all probability as well as fact; and some of them, as I have been assured, even in the presence of your Grace. His meanings and his movements were indeed peevish enough, but his words were not. He threatened me with nothing but his pen, yet owned he had no pretence to wit. And indeed I am heartily glad, for his own sake, that he proceeded no further; for, the least uproar would have called his nearest neighbours, first to my assistance, and next to the manifest danger of his life. And I would not willingly have even a dog killed upon my account. Ever since, he hath amused himself with declaring, in all companies, especially before bishops, and lords, and members of Parliament, his resolutions for vengeance, and the several manners by which he will put it in execution. It is only to the advice of some judicious friends that your Grace owes the trouble of this letter. For, though I may be dispirited enough by sickness and years, yet I have little reason to apprehend any danger from that man; and those who seem to have most regard for my safety, are no more apprehensive than myself, especially such as best know his character. For his very enemies, and even his ridiculers, who are, of the two, by far the greater number, allow him to be a peaceable man in all things except his words, his rhetorical action, his looks, and his hatred to the clergy; which however are all known, by abundance of experience, to be perfectly harmless, and particularly as to the clergy. I do not doubt, but, if he will be so good to continue stedfast in his principles and practices, he may at proper junctures contribute very much to the honour and interests of that reverend body, as well as employ and improve the wit of many young gentlemen in the city, the university and the rest of the kingdom'.

If Swift was dispirited, as he claims, 'by sickness and years', it did not prevent his launching into yet another malicious lampoon directed against Bettesworth. This one, entitled *The Yahoo's Overthrow: Or the Kevan Bayl's New Ballad, upon Serjeant Kite's Insulting the Dean*,[52] is addressed to the 'Jolly boys of St. Kevans, St. Patricks, Donore and Smithfield'. Dr. Elrington Ball notes that Kevan Bayle was a cant term for the rabble of this District of Dublin. It was to them, therefore, that Swift announced –

> 'Bow B – – – th, that booby, and S – – – l[53] in grain,
> Hath insulted us all by insulting the Dean'.[54]

In addition to using such epithets as 'booby', 's——l' (scoundrel, 'skip of a lawyer', 'pedlar', 'slave', Swift charges that –

> 'He only the rights of the clergy debates,
> Their rights! their importance! We'll set on new rates
> On their Tythes at half-nothing, their priesthood at less':[55]

Swift criticises Bettesworth's lack of legal ability, his morals, his rhet'ric, bombast, silly jests, and recounted his meeting with Bettesworth –

> 'He began as he bragged, with a rant and a roar,
> He bragg'd how he bounc'd and he swore how he swore'.[56]

Then Swift went on to assure him that –

> '…whene'er we can hit,
> We'll show him the way how to crop and to slit',[57]

and prophesied that –

> 'When all this is over we'll make him amends,
> To the Dean he shall go; they shall kiss, and be friends'.[58]

And, once again, as in the case of Whitshed, and anticipating similar objections, Swift answers –

> 'If you say this is hard, on a man that is reckon'd
> That Serjeant at law, whom we call Kite the Second,
> You mistake; for a Slave, who will coax his superiors,
> May be proud to be licking a great man's posteriors'.[59]

At that time, William Dunkin,[60] who had impressed Swift with his translation of *Carberiae Rupes*, and whom Swift had assisted in many ways, and sought to advance and obtain him various livings, proceeded to attack Bettesworth in a lampoon entitled *Bettesworth's Exultation* – Upon Hearing that his Name would be Transmitted to Posterity in Dr. Swift's Works'.[61] Dunkin had no reason to attack Bettesworth, unless, as a member of the clergy, he resented Bettesworth's attitude in the House towards the Petition, or unless he was anxious to curry further favour with Swift. In the course of his attack, he attributed to Bettesworth a feeling of elation upon being lampooned by the Dean –

> 'For had he not pointed me out, I had slept till
> E'en doomsday, a poor insignificant reptile;
> Half lawyer, half actor, pert, dull and inglorious,
> Obscure, and unheard of – but now I'm notorious'.

Dunkin sneers –

> 'Though my title is spurious, why should I be dastard,
> A man is a man, though he should be a bastard'.

He calls Bettesworth 'a well painted monkey', and concludes with –

> 'The Scriptures affirm (as I heard in my youth,
> For indeed I ne'er read them, to speak for once truth)

That death is the wages of sin, but the just
Shall die not, although they be laid in the dust.
They say so; so be it, I care not a straw,
Although I'd be dead, both in gospel and law,
In verse I shall live, and be read in each climate,
What more can be said of prime serjeant or primate?'

We have already noted the intervention of 'Pickle Herring'[62] of Cork,
who must be regarded as reporting, as well as satirising, upon Bettesworth's
discomfiture in Cork and elsewhere, when he said –

'Is it not sufficient to see him so unmasked and stigmatised, that he can
no longer be a tool even for a Court sharper, and, what is worst of all
for him, no longer to be in pay with them? Is it not sufficient for all to
see his poor skull (God help it!) incurably bumped and bulged by that
damnable bounce of his against the pulpit cornice? Is it not sufficient to
see with what pain and shame he wriggles along by that confounded
splinter of the bar, he lately got thrust into his – and which has left him
a running sore to his dying day? Is it not sufficient to see him, all the last
term, walk about in merry sadness, an idle spectator in the Courts,
where he was not retained even for his most noted talent of dirt-flinger...
Is it not sufficient to see him doubly tormented in putting a good
countenance on treatment which is inwardly gnawing and consuming
him...? Is it not sufficient to see him... everywhere he goes, the common butt of jibe, wink and titter? Is it not sufficient, that after what has
been flying about since he left it, he knows not how to show his face in
town, nor how to stand the infinite mortifications he is to meet with
this Winter? Is it not sufficient that, as his case stands, it is the Serjeant
against all the world, and all the world against the Serjeant?

Thus far, Swift and his friends had triumphed over and discomfited
Bettesworth. We do not know what advice, if any, Bettesworth sought,
or from whom. It may, well, be that when the heat of passion subsided,
he realised that weapons other than his pen or his penknife were needed to
discomfit the Dean. It seems to us that he, or someone advising him, had
studied the past history of the Dean, to find out, so to speak, what was his
Achilles' heel. Time was on Bettesworth's side. Swift and his faction,
elated with success, appear to have thrown caution to the winds, and

provided Bettesworth with his first opportunity to hit back. On March 3rd 1735 Bettesworth, moving as a member of the Irish House of Commons, struck Swift a deadly blow as appears from the following record:

> 'A complaint being made to the House of a printed Pamphlet entituled 'A New Proposal for the Better Regulation and Improvement of Quadrille' wherein are two scandalous paragraphs highly reflecting on a Member of this House, and it appearing by Evidence that the said Pamphlet was published and sold by George Faulkner, Printer, in Essex Street,
>
> Ordered that the said George Faulkner be, for his said offence, taken into the custody of the Serjeant-at-Arms attending this House.[63]
>
> George Faulkner, Printer, in custody of the Serjeant-at-Arms, was brought to the Bar, and examined touching the Pamphlet... and the Pamphlet being produced to him, he there owned that he had printed and published the same.
>
> Ordered that the said George Faulkner be for his said offence committed close prisoner to Newgate and that Mr. Speaker do issue his Warrant accordingly'.[64]

The circumstances surrounding this resounding Bettesworth move were as follows: On February 23rd 1735-36 Josiah Hort sent Swift a manuscript which contained 'a skit upon the then fashionable game of cards called quadrille'. There is no doubt from the terms of Hort's letter[65] that Swift was in collusion with Hort in the composition of the work: 'I fear you will find the addition, pursuant to your hint, heavy... I hope you will supply what shall be wanting of spirit'.[66] There is no doubt, also, that its purpose was to further denigrate Bettesworth; for it was part of the theme to suggest that where dispute arose between ladies playing the game of quadrille, Bettesworth should be employed as Arbitrator and, 'if any Lady should find herself aggrieved by the decision of the said S-rj-t B-; it shall be lawful to remove her cause by Appeal before the upright man in Essex Street'. Hort urged that 'you will supply what shall be wanting of spirit; and when you have pruned the rough feathers, the Ands and Thats, etc., you will send the Kite[67] to the Faulconer[68] to set it aflying'. The fact that Faulkner was committed to Newgate seems to have gravely shaken Swift, who appears ever since the Whiteshed incident to have had a terror of his printers being prosecuted – 'My printers have been twice prosecuted, to

88

my great expense, on account of discourses I write for the public service'[69] and, because of his experiences with Whitshed, was 'determined henceforth never to be the instrument of leaving an innocent man at the mercy of that Bench'.[70] There were reasons, too, why Faulkner's committal to Newgate frightened Swift still more. Dr. Maurice Craig tells us that Newgate was replaced by a newer Newgate in 1773, and he makes it clear that life in the Dublin prisons of the eighteenth century presented scenes of incredible depravity and riot.[71] Indeed, the conditions in old Newgate, upon Faulkner being committed, must have been deadly serious, because on March 5th 1735,[72] Faulkner petitioned the House of Commons, and referred to his 'very bad state of health' and 'that at present there is a malignant Fever in the said Jail'. Once again, Swift provides a picture of the turmoil which the committal created in his mind, and he elaborates upon this, and upon the suffering of Faulkner, in a letter which he wrote to Hort[73] – '...to tell you my thoughts upon the affair of the poor printer, who suffered so much upon your Lordship's account, confined to a dungeon among common thieves, and others with infectious diseases, to the hazard of his life; besides the expense of above twenty-five pounds, and besides the ignominy to be sent to Newgate like a Common male-factor'. Swift's concern and distress is patent to all. Obviously, Bettesworth had found the best way to revenge himself upon Swift. Bettesworth believed that Swift was the author of Quadrille, and no doubt, if Faulkner weakened and disclosed Swift's name, we woud have had one of the greatest confrontations before the Bar of the House of Commons ever recorded. Not for the first time, however, Swift owed his liberty to his printer. In spite of his sufferings, Faulkner did not weaken. He declined to divulge the author's name. Instead, on March 9th 1735, he again came before the House 'expressing his sorrow for his offence, and begging pardon... and praying to be discharged', Whereupon it was ordered 'that the said George Faulkner be discharged out of custody paying fees'.[74] In his letter to Hort, Swift stresses the financial situation of Faulkner, and acknowledges that his work 'although it be written with spirit and humour, yet, if had not affected Bettesworth, would scarce have cleared above a shilling to Faulkner; neither would he have done it at all but at my urgency'.[75] But Bettesworth moved on firmer ground, and the Dean was on the retreat. Bettesworth had begun to strike back and perhaps was about to sound 'a blast from the proper trumpet'.

Notes

1. *Personal Sketches of His Own Times* (3rd Edit.) Vol. 1, p. 219: George Rout-ledge & Sons, London 1869.
2. *The First Satire of The Second Book of Horace Imitated* ll. 83-84.
3. R. Halsband, author of *The Life of Lady Mary Wortley Montagu* (Oxford Paper-backs, 1961) p. 143 discusses the authorship of *Verses Address'd to the Imitator of the First Satire of the Second Book of Horace*, which Lady Mary Wortley Montagu had denied, but who owned 'the design was so well meant, and so excellently executed that I cannot be sorry they were written'.
4. Barrington, ibid. p. 220.
5. *Thoughts on Various Subjects*, included in '*Satires and Personal Writings*' by Jonathan Swift, ed. by William Alfred Eddy, p. 406: (London, Oxford University Press, 1962).
6. Letter to Alexander Pope, Sept. 29th 1725. Corr. (Williams) Vol. 3, p. 102.
7. Ibid. p. 103.
8. *A Panegyric on Dean Swift*: Poems, Vol. 2, p. 498 ll. 167-168.
9. *Verses on the Death of Dean Swift*, ibid. p. 571, ll. 455-458.
10. *Epistle To A Lady*, ibid. p. 634, ll. 153-154.
11. Ibid. ll. 177-180.
12. *Prose Works* (Davis), Vol. 9, pp.13-32.
13. *Letter to Alexander Pope*, 10th Jan. 1721. Corr. (Williams) Vol. 2, p. 367.
14. Ibid. pp. 367-368.
15. *Whitshed's Motto on His Coach*: Poems, Vol. 1, p. 348, ll.1-4.
16. *Verses On The Upright Judge, Who Condemned The Drapier's Printer*: Poems, ibid. p. 349.
17. *On The Same*: ibid. p. 349.
18. *A Short View of the State of Ireland*, Prose Works (Davis), Vol. 12, p. 8.
19. *An Answer To a Paper Called a Memorial*, Prose Works (Davis) Vol. 12, p. 23.
20. *A Serious Poem Upon William Wood*, Poems, Vol. 1, p. 334, ll. 1-6.
21. Ibid. ll. 25-28.
22. For the most of this information I am indebted to the following: Dr. F. J. E. Hurst, Librarian, Trinity College Dublin, Brigadier Maurice D. Jephson, Mallow, Co. Cork, and to his invaluable work *An Anglo-Irish Miscellany* (Allan Figgis, Dublin, 1964); *Mallow and Some Mallow Men* by Henry J. Twiss (J.C.A.H.S. Vol. 31, p. 65, 2nd series): *Cork M.P.s 1559-1800* by Dorothea Townshend (J.C.A.H.S. Vol. 1, p. 117).
23. *Correspondence of Jonathan Swift*, Vol. 5, p. 54, n. ed. Elrington Ball (G. Bell & Sons Ltd., London 1913).
24. *The Sobriquet* says Ball (ibid. Appendix IV, p. 446) 'used by the writer perhaps

finds to-day its best equivalent in the term merry-andrew. It was first applied early in the seventeenth century as the name of a humorous character in a German play, and was afterwards adopted by the Dutch, whose use of it has been made famous by Addison in *The Spectator*.

25. Ibid. p. 447.
26. *A Proposal For The Universal Use of Irish Manufacture* Vol. 9, p. 21.
27. Ibid.
28. Journal of the House of Commons of Ireland, Vol. 3, p. 358.
29. Landa, pp. 98–99.
30. Prose Works (Davis), Vol. 9, pp.45–66.
31. Ibid. p. 48.
32. Prose Works (Davis) Vol. 12, pp. 179–186, and 191–202.
33. *On The Irish Bishops*: Poems, Vol. 3, p. 804, ll. 29–32.
34. Ibid. ll. 17–18.
35. Journal of the House of Commons of Ireland, Vol. 4, p. 99 (1731–1748).
36. Journal of the House of Commons of Ireland, Vol. 3, p. 439.
37. Prose Works (Davis) Vol. 13, pp. 93–105 and 105–107 – 'One terrible circumstance in this Bill, is that of turning the Tyth of Flax and Hemp into what Lawyers call a Modus, or a certain sum in lieu of a tenth Part of the product'. (p. 101).
38. Journal of the House of Commons of Ireland, Dec. 24th 1733. Vol. 4, p. 110.
39. 'The House of Commons always had the right to prohibit the publication of proceedings in their House. The House of Commons of the Long Parliament was the first to forbid a member 'to give a copy or publish in print anything that he shall speak here without leave of the House'. Such reporting as did take place was, entirely, unofficial. It is interesting to note that when Samuel Johnson wrote the series of debates which appeared in the Gentleman's Magazine in 1740-3, he took as his model Swift's Senate debates in Lilliput. T. C. Hansard was first the printer and later publisher of an unofficial series of Parliamentary debates inaugurated by William Cobbett in 1803. In 1909 the government took over the responsibility for reporting and the production of the debates was placed with the Stationery Office'. (The Law and Custom of the Constitution', Sir William Anson; Chambers Encyclopaedia, Vol. VI, Life of Samuel Johnson and Boswell, and other sources). If we do not know what Bettesworth said, we have some idea of what Counsel for the Petitioners may have said, because it is suggested that 'Some Further Reasons Against the Bill for settling the Tyth of Hemp, Flax. etc' (see note 37) may have been adopted by Swift from the contents of the Brief held by Counsel on the hearing of the Petition. (As to this, see Landa, p. 127, n. 1).
40. Poems, Vol. 3, p. 810.
41. Correspondence, Vol. 5 (ed. Elrington Ball) p. 54.
42. 'There appears to have been no malicious or deliberate intention to weaken the Church; the legislation was in fact part of repeated efforts to develop and maintain a flourishing linen industry in Ireland... The point relevant for our purpose is that the pending legislation of 1733 was not conceived as a penalty inflicted on the clergy'. Landa, pp. 124-125.
43. Poems, Vol. 3, p. 810.
44. Some evidence as to this is supplied by the following entry in the Journal of the Irish House of Commons for March 14th 1729, p. 638. 'Ordered that Richard Bettesworth Esq., a member of this House have leave to absent himself for a fortnight for recovery of his health'.
45. Poems, Vol. 3, pp. 809-813.

46. Ibid. p. 811, ll. 11-14.
47. Ibid. p. 812. ll. 25-28.
48. Ibid. p. 812. ll. 33-36.
49. *Life of Swift*, Thomas Sheridan, p. 438.
50. January 1733-4: Corr. (Williams) Vol. 4, pp. 220/221.
51. Swift, as has been suggested, was, most likely, present in the House of Commons when Counsel argued his Petition against the Bill already referred to. If this were so, then surely he must have seen and heard Bettesworth speak, in which event his denial that he did not know him, and his pretence of innocence do not add to his credibility.
52. Poems, Vol. 3, pp. 814-817.
53. *Scoundrel.* Sheridan, 1784, supplies the word in full. Sir H. Williams at Poems, Vol. 3, p. 814 note.
54. Ibid. ll. 3-4.
55. Ibid. ll. 31-33.
56. Ibid. ll. 43-44.
57. Ibid. ll. 51-52.
58. Ibid. ll. 61-62.
59. Ibid. ll. 66-69.
60. Sir Harold Williams – Corr. Vol. 4, pp. 544-545 tells us that the date of Swift's personal acquaintanceship with Dunkin is in doubt, but that after publication of 'Bettesworth's Exultation' Swift began to take an interest in the young man's fortunes.
61. The Poems of Jonathan Swift D.D. p. 254, ed. William Ernest Browning (T. Bell & Sons Ltd., London) 1910.
62. Infra note 24.
63. Journal of the Irish House of Commons, Vol. 4, pp. 211-214.
64. Ibid.
65. Corr. (Williams) Vol. 4, p. 461.
66. Ibid.
67. Bettesworth was known as Serjeant Kite.
68. George Faulkner, Swift's printer.
69. *An Answer to Several Letters sent me from Unknown Hands.* Prose Works (Davis) Vol. 12, p. 85.
70. Ibid.
71. *Dublin 1660-1860* by Maurice Craig (Cressett Press).
72. Journal of the Irish House of Commons, Vol. 4, infra p. 213.
73. Corr. (Williams) Vol. 4, pp. 482-483: Letter dated May 12th 1736.
74. Journal of the Irish House of Commons, infra p. 214.
75. Corr. (Williams) Vol. 4, p. 483.

The matter of the Freedom of Cork

A little more than twelve months had passed since Richard Bettesworth had succeeded in having George Faulkner committed to Newgate to the great discomfiture of Swift, when a motion was moved at a meeting of the Corporation of Cork to confer the Freedom of the City on the Dean. It was Copper coins,[1] not Gold, which secured for Swift the Freedom of the City of Dublin.[2] It was Gold, not Copper, which secured him the Freedom of Cork. When in 1736 Archbishop Boulter proposed to reduce the value of the guinea and to import a quantity of Copper Coin from England, Swift opposed both measures – 'The Drapier went this day to the Tholsel as a Merchant, to sign a Petition to the Government against lowering Gold, where we hear he made a long speech, for which he will be reckoned a Jacobite'.[3] At the same time, the Corporation of Cork expressed its apprehension, 'that a reduction of the Gold coin is designed'[4] and its opinion 'that it will be of the utmost prejudice to the Kingdom in general, for all our country goods must inevitably fall in proportion to the reduction, besides it will certainly carry away all our gold and prevent any more being brought to us'.[5] Within a further five days, 'our Representatives having enclosed to Mr. Mayor four Schemes which were handed about in Dublin for reducing the value of Gold coin, which we think would be prejudicial and there being a pamphlet entitled *A Scheme of the Money Matters of Ireland*, printed in Dublin in 1729, and desire that our Representatives will order 400 of said pamphlet to be reprinted and a book to be given to each of the Members of Parliament, the remainder to be sent down'.[6] Thus, the Drapier who had become on the defeat of Woods 'in great Repute, the Darling of the populace: his image and superscription on a great many sign-posts in this City and other great Towns'[7] became, also, 'the Idol of the Court of Aldermen'[8] in Cork. Some corroboration is provided by a letter written from Corke by Rev. Christopher Donnellan to Swift, who assures him 'That they' (Corkmen) 'are not such Brutes as to be insensible to the Dean's Merit; ever since we came down this Town and Country has rung of yr praises, for opposing reduction of Coin, and they look upon stop that is likely to be put to that Affair, as a second Deliverance they owe you'.[9]

The picture painted by the Earl of Orrery and Rev. Christopher Donnellan[10] calls for examination. This must depend on a reconstruction of the known facts, an examination of the letters of Orrery and Donnellan, and some conjecture. Let us, therefore, consider the form of resolution which was presented to the Corporation of Cork on the 20th Jan. 1736. First, the resolution was an omnibus one in which the names of some sixteen persons, thirteen of whom had served as Apprentices to Citizens and were entitled, as of right, to be admitted to the Freedom of the City, were submitted to the Corporation. Secondly, with Swift were proposed two other Clergymen, the Dean of Cork[11] and the Dean of Cloyne,[12] who at that time were Deans Elect of Cork and Cloyne, and it was usual to confer the Freedom of the City on distinguished members of the Clergy in such circumstances. Only the timing of the proposal, so far as it concerned them, is suspect. The resolution may now be examined. Caulfield carefully extracted it from the Records of the Cork Corporation [13] where it appeared in the following form:

That Parr Thompson, having served Wm Thompson, be admitted free; likewise Thomas, only son of Jas. Weekes; Trayer Lawton, having served Mr. Benjn. Lawton; James Cox Esq.; Daniel, only son of Ald. Dan Pearse; Abraham Chatterton, Distiller; John, only son of Rice Wight; Robert, eldest son of Wm. Long; Benj. Wetherall, paying £5; Devereux Spratt, having served Ald. Delahoid; Richard Moore – Thomas Bateman, having served Ald. Delahoid; Isaac Busiy, having served Math. Ardouin; Revd. Deane Jonathan Swift in a Silver Box; Revd. Willm. Meade, Dean of Cork; Revd. Isaac Goldsmyth, Deane of Cloyne.[14]

If the formal resolution thus cited stood alone, it would be difficult to read much into it. There is, however, more: The record of the meeting contains an unusual addendum which, it is submitted, was inserted into the minute either after the meeting had ended or at a subsequent meeting, before the Mayor signed the minutes of the Corporation meeting of 20th Jan. 1736. This addendum, transcribed by Caulfield, is as follows:

'We dissent to the freedom of Dean Swift – Danl. Engain, Joseph Austin, Augustus Carrée'.[15]

It is important to note the difference between the manner in which the motion is recorded, and the dissent. The motion is shown as a simple statement, while the dissent is entered in the Record under quotation marks. What is more significant, however, and suspicious, is that the record of names of those attending the meeting discloses that neither Danl. Engain or Augustus Carrée were present. The attendance was as follows: Mr. Mayor, Sher. Crone and Bradshaw; Alden. Knapp, Hawkins, Bennett, Atkins, Millerd, Austin, Huleatt, Croker; Mr. Owgan, Travers, Dring, and Fuller c.s.[16] Nor is there anything to suggest that Alderman Joseph Austin had made any objection during the discussion which followed the motion. The next meeting of the Corporation took place on 19th Feb. 1736,[17] at which the three dissenters were present. It is more than likely that the dissent was made at that meeting, and that advantage was taken of what was subsequently claimed to be a long-standing practice, to avail of the right to do so. That a dispute arose touching upon this practice if, in fact, it was followed, appears from a meeting of the Corporation which took place on 13th Sept. 1736, some five months later, as follows:

'It has been the constant practice when any affair was proposed to the Council it was adjourned to the next Council. Ordered, that said practice continue, and when any affair is proposed, if any one member seconded by another desires the debate to be adjourned, it be adjourned, provided the said Council be not held within eight days after, the Mayor to signify that the affair is to be considered',[18]

but if this was the basis on which the dissent was made, then it seems that the correct procedure was followed. It would also seem that Alderman Austin,[19] who was at both meetings, may have been prevailed upon to change his mind in the month that followed. It is significant that on April 11th 1736, Dr. Edward Barry writes from Cork to Lord Orrery, and notes – 'Our town is crowded with Lawyers and country Gentlemen; agistment is the word which unites their Hopes and Fears... I saw here Serj. Bettesworth'[20] and what is most significant is that a veil of silence was drawn by the Corporation over its deliberations and internal difficulties, and several months were, deliberately, allowed to pass before any formal notification of the Freedom conferred upon him was given to the Dean. We endeavour to enquire, therefore, into the reason for the dissent, and as to why there was delay in communicating the Freedom to the Dean.

Only one shadow clouded Swift's reputation – Vanessa, whose death[21] does not seem to have aroused any strong public expression of feeling in her favour. 'No discernible ripple disturbed the surface of the strange domestic arrangements of the Deanery during the years that followed'.[22] Vanessa's instruction to her executors (if she ever gave it) that her correspondence with Swift should be printed and published was circumvented by the intervention of powerful forces.[23] By April 19th, 1727, however, clouds, which had been gathering for some time, became dark when copies of 'Cadenus and Vanessa',[24] a poem which Swift had written, and in which he described their friendship, were passed around.[25] In spite of Swift's apparent unconcern, he was sensitive and apprehensive.[26] The poem contained lines from which serious inferences regarding his relationship with Vanessa could be drawn.[27] It is significant that early editions of the poem omitted these lines. Soon, however, a second edition included them, and so did successive editions published elsewhere. Then in January 1735, twelve months before the Freedom motion was introduced before the Corporation, and shortly before Bettesworth moved to commit George Faulkner for contempt, Faulkner published the first standard edition of the Dean's works.[28] It does not appear that Swift's relationship with Vanessa made any impression on the members of the Cork Corporation. The powerful, influential merchant class of Cork, with its many Dublin and country connections, must have been aware of Swift's association with Vanessa, and of his flight to Myross: But, could it have been used as an additional argument against his fitness to be a Freeman of Cork? We have no proof that it was. It is certain that there was not only a pro-Swift, but also an anti-Swift, party in Cork, and that Swift had enemies in Cork. He had insulted, reviled and affronted the merchants of Cork by insisting that instead of 'being dealers' they had become 'peddlers and cheats'.[29] Richard Bettesworth, of an influential Cork family, had every reason to hate Swift. We suggest that he would have been likely to do everything within his power to prevent Swift from receiving any honour from the Corporation of Cork or, if he was not strong enough to do this, then to bring about the denigration of the Dean in the manner of its giving. Perhaps it was hoped by Swift's friends, on January 20th 1736, that by coupling the names of the Deans of Cork and Cloyne with that of Jonathan Swift, the Alder-

Skiddy's Alms House

men and Burgesses would be forced, if scandal was to be avoided, to accept all three as Freemen, rather than excluding one and accepting the others? That Swift regarded, or suspected, Bettesworth's complicity in the events which occurred is strongly suggested in his correspondence with Lord Orrery, in which he openly states – 'My Fear is what I dare not mention, that they could not find a Messenger who had honesty enough to bring it, except Mr. Bettesworth'.[30]

It will be noticed that notwithstanding the fact that the Freedom had been conferred on Jan. 20th 1736, that Orrery had written the Dean on March 15th 1736, and Rev. Christopher Donnellan had written him on July 2nd 1736 – a period of almost six months – no formal notification of the Freedom had been sent by the Cork Corporation to Swift. We offer the view, from internal evidence afforded by the correspondence, and by subsequent events, that the Swift opposition had proved so strong as to succeed in limiting the form and manner in which the Freedom was to be presented, in that no inscription would be placed on the box, and that the parchment accompanying it should not contain any reference to the reasons which had induced the Cork Corporation to grant it. Here, we remind our Readers of the close parallel which exists between the treatment meted out to Swift in Dublin when the Freedom of that City was offered to him;[31] for on that occasion Joshua, Lord Allen, had objected with 'My lord, you and your city can squander away the public money in giving a gold box to a fellow who hath libelled the government'[32] and had succeeded in delaying the presentation of the Freedom box for a considerable time, and then without an inscription. It would be unusual if this was not known in Cork, and particularly to Bettesworth. We suggest, also, that the Mayor had refused to communicate the form which the 'Freedom' had taken to the Dean, because he had reason to anticipate the Dean's bitter reaction.

Caulfield's records make it clear that the Cork Corporation had special representatives in Dublin, whose duty it was to look after the affairs and petitions, and other projects of the Corporation there, and to represent the Mayor in making presentations and attendances at functions. Yet, if silence means anything, it would appear either that the Mayor had refused to nominate any member of the Corporation to attend on the Dean with his Silver Box and Freedom, or that efforts to find a willing and suitable representative were proceeding cautiously and slowly. When Christopher Donnellan wrote his letter assuring the Dean that Cork people 'were not such brutes'[33] or insensible of his merit, there is no reason one can find for his having written in this way, unless, as a newcomer to the City, and a friend, like Orrery, of Swift, he was asked to assuage the Dean's anger, and to mitigate the insult which the form of the Freedom and manner of its presentation would offer. This, perhaps, explains why the Earl of Orrery, then one of Swift's great friends, writes his letter.[34] He had, only, returned to Cork, and he writes as if he had, suddenly, discovered something new and pleasant. He writes, first of some of the things which, perhaps, Swift would like to hear of Cork – 'Unfurnished with variety, and drooping under the natural dullness of the place. Materials for a letter are as hard to be found, as Money, Sense, Honesty or Truth – But I'll write on...'[35] This hoped-for acceptable opening gambit concluded, he proceeds to prepare the Dean for the formal announcement of his freedom, and for the obvious disappointment which a Silver box and the attendant background events would mean to him. 'I have not yett been upon the Change but am told that you are the Idol of the Court of Aldermen. They have sent you your Freedom'.[36] If Orrery had been 'upon the Change', where the meeting of the Corporation took place, then he must have heard the gossip which, undoubtedly, followed upon the dissenters' action; and, if he were not, then his informant either deliberately withheld the information, or as we suspect, Orrery and Donnellan had been approached by the Mayor, or on his behalf, and asked to help in getting the Cork Corporation and the Mayor out of their difficulty. In our view, Orrery was briefed, and this view finds some support in his next statement, which offers a 'classical' explanation as to why a Silver, and not a Gold, box was to be the receptacle in which the Freedom parchment was contained – 'The most learned of them having read a most dreadful Account in Littleton's Dictionary of Pandora's Gold Box, it was unanimously agreed not to venture so valuable a present in so dangerous a metal. Had these sage Counsellors consider'd that Pandora was a woman... they would have seen that the ensuing Evil arose from the Sex, and not from the Ore – But, I shall speak with more certainty of these Affairs when I have taken my Seat among the Greybeards'.[37] Swift, however, is not deceived. He knows far more than Orrery appreciates – Swift replies: – First he explains – 'The Thing was this. A great Flood of Halfpence from England hath rolled in upon us by the Politicks of the Primate. I rayled at them to Faulkner, who printed an Advertisement naming me and my ill will towards them... I quarrell not at the Coin, but at the Indignity of not being coyned here, and the loss of 12000 in gold and silver to us'.[38] Then he makes it quite clear that he is, already, aware of events in Cork. 'I am told by others as well as Yr Lordship, that the City of Cork hath sent me my Silver box and Freedom; but, I know nothing of it'.[39] Then he rails at Orrery – 'When I get my Cork box I shall certainly sell it for not being Gold'[40] and rejects the explanation that Orrery offered for the choice of a Silver box; 'I have consulted the Pantheon and do not find your Account of Pandora's box to be authentick. Littleton mentions nothing of the metal'.[41] Therefore, Swift insists, 'I desire your Alderm^n would begin with Gold, and if any mischief should happen, let them send another 18 times and 50 grains heavier in Silver'.[42] He sneers at the suggestion that Orrery should take his seat among the Greybeards – 'Taken your seat among them! Pray my Lord are you an Alderman of Cork? or, do you speak it out of Vanity?'[43] Swift then discusses various items of general news; but, it is clear that he wants Orrery to know that he (Swift) knows more than Orrery thought. He returns again to the 'Freedom' and the 'box', insisting – 'I must repeat again, that I am told by others as well as your Lordship of my Freedom and box being already come and delivered to me; so that I am the onely ignorant person',[44] and then he hints at what he fears, and as a tail-piece he mentions the man who is uppermost in his mind – 'My Fear is what I dare not mention, that they could not find a Messenger who had honesty enough to bring it, except Mr. Bettesworth'.[45] The message is quite clear – the Corporation of Cork had set out to insult him: The person responsible for the insult was that same 'Booby Bettesworth' whom he, Swift, had libelled, who had followed him to a friend's house and threatened him, and who (if he contrived the insult or not) was ready to return to his house and present it to the Dean. Swift, with his knowledge of Irish Parliamentary procedure and of the practice of public bodies, knew that the Cork Corporation had Representatives in Dublin. He, surely, was aware of the procedure followed less than a year previously by the Cork Corporation, when on the 30th Jan. 1735 it was decided 'That his Grace the Duke of Dorset, Lord Lieutenant of this Kingdom' (to whom Swift had written an account of Bettesworth's call and the scene which had followed) 'be presented with his Freedom in a Gold box and that Mr. Mayor desire Hugh Dickson and Eman Pigot Esq. our representatives, to wait on his Grace to beg acceptance of the same, and of our humblest thanks for his great goodness and favour to this City'.[46] It is noticeable that, following Swift's reply, henceforward Orrery makes no further reference to Swift's freedom in the letters which pass between them, and lapses into silence. He, at least, had done his best. What Swift's answer to Donnellan's assurance[47] was we do not know.

Thesituation, instead of improving, had worsened. The Cork Corporation was now in a very delicate position. Orrery and Donnellan had failed. The Dean's attitude, instead of softening, had hardened, and he was demanding a Gold instead of a Silver box, and delivery by a suitable messenger. We have already suggested that the Corporation's search for a messenger acceptable to the Dean was a slow but careful one. The ideal man was, at all times, to hand, but it was neither his duty nor his privilege to act as messenger, and indeed, he must have given long, careful and heart-searching thought before he finally agreed to act, and when he communicated with the Dean, he did so gingerly and cautiously, as appears from Swift's letter of Aug. 15th 1737 to the Corporation –

'Gentlemen, I received from you some weeks ago the Honour of my Freedom in a Silver box at the hands of Mr. Stannard, but, it was not delivered to me in as many weeks more, because, I suppose he was too full of more important Business'.[48]

Eaton Stannard of Tubber, Co.Dublin, had all the qualifications of the ideal messenger. He was a Corkman, the son of George Stannard of Ballyhealey, Co.Cork. He was M.P. for Midleton, Co.Cork, until his decease in 1755. He was a Barrister-at-Law, and on April 12th 1728, Cork honoured him by appointing him Recorder of Cork in the place of the Rt. Hon. John Brodrick.[49] This was an unusual honour, because at that time, Stannard was Recorder of Dublin. He could not hold the two posts, and therefore declined the offer of the Cork office. It appears to have been customary to grant the Freedom of Cork to the Recorder for the time being. Stannard must have been very popular among the Aldermen and Burgesses of the Cork Corporation; because notwithstanding his refusal to accept the Recordership, his friends proceeded, not without opposition, to nominate him as a Freeman of the City. The motion came before the Corporation on the 7th May 1728 – 'The question being put whether Eaton Stannard Esq., should be admitted a Freeman at large, carried by a majority of 4 in 14 to admit him'.[50] Thus, he was a man who by his local ties, parliamentary obligations, and by the honours offered and conferred upon him, owed something to Cork. More important, he was a close confidant and friend of Swift, to whom he had rendered generous service.[51] Swift thought so highly of Stannard that he invited him to become one of the executors and trustees of his Will.[52] One of the most tantalising disappointments is that we do not know what Swift said to Eaton Stannard when he called upon him with the Freedom box and parchment, but, it is reasonable to assume that whatever it was, Stannard remained in Swift's good graces, and having discharged his duty, must have declined to deliver Swift's reply. But the Dean, in selecting his messenger to deliver his reply to the Cork Corporation, was equally subtle. Was it chance or coincidence that this person chosen was George Faulkner, the man whom Bettesworth had committed to Newgate? 'Mr. Faulkner will be the bearer of my letter, who sets out this morning for Corke'.[53] And what of the letter itself? It will be seen from an examination of the contents that Swift's mind must have turned to the events which followed the refusal of the Dublin Corporation to give him his Dublin Freedom in a Gold box. Let us, once more, turn to these events. What Swift said then is preserved in a remarkable document which he wrote, and left for us to read. And there can be no doubt, from a comparison of this with his letter to the Mayor of Cork, that when Swift sat down to write the Cork Corporation, he had his 'Substance of what was said by the Dean'[54] before him – 'That it was true, this honour was mingled with a little mortification, by the delay which attended it... with acknowledging to have expressed his wishes, that an inscription might have been graven on the box, showing some reason why the city thought fit to do him that honour, which was much out of the common forms to a person in a private station; those distinctions being usually made only to chief governors, or persons in very high employments'.[55] When he writes the Mayor of Cork, Swift's bitterness and resentment overflow – 'I could have wished as I am a private man, that in the Instrument of my Freedom, you had pleased to assign your Reasons for making choice of me. I know it is a usual Compliment to bestow the Freedom of a City on an Archbishop or Lord-Chancellor, and other persons in great Titles, merely on Account of their Stations or Power: But a private Man, and a perfect Stranger, without Power or Grandeur, may justly expect to find the Motives assigned in the Instrument of his Freedom, on what Account he is thus distinguished. And, yet I cannot discover in the whole Parchment Scrip one reason offered'.[56] Without pretence, mercilessly and bitterly, Swift challenges the Corporation to explain the lack of an inscription on the box: 'Next, as to the Silver Box, there is not so much as my name upon it, or any one Syllable to show it was a Present from your City'.[57] Then, with masterly contempt, and superb generalship, he returns the insult and, at the same time, forces the Corporation of Cork into a corner and leaves it to resolve his challenge and its dilemma with: 'Therefore, I have by the Advice of Friends, agreeing with my Opinion, sent back the Box, and Instrument of Freedom by Mr. Faulkner, to be returned to you; leaving to your Choice, whether to insert the Reasons for which you were pleased to give me my Freedom, or bestow the Box upon some more worthy Person, whom you may have an Intention to Honour, because it will equally fit everybody'.[58] And he, sarcastically, signs himself – 'with true Esteem and Gratitude Gentlemen, your Obedient and obliged Servant'.[59] A month was to pass before a reply was sent to Swift on September 14th, 1737,[60] signed by Thomas Farren, Mayor. The records of the Corporation are, completely, silent as to whether Swift's letter was placed before it or, if it was, what ruling was made.[61] Farren makes statements which, if correct, we would expect to have found recorded. No such record appears. We can only surmise and suggest that in the intervening period, Farren took counsel of individual members before the form of his letter was, finally, drafted and settled. He opens it cautiously, and expresses his sorrow that 'the health of a man, the whole kingdom has at heart should be so much in danger'.[62] He, shamelessly, suggests that the blame for the omission to inform the Dean of the reasons which had prompted the Corporation to honour him with his Freedom must rest, partly, on Eaton Stannard because 'when the Box with your Freedom was given the Recorder, to be presented to you, I hoped that he would in the name of the City, have expressed their grateful acknowledgments for the many services the publick has received from you, which are the motives that induced us to make you one of our citizens'.[63] He then explains the matter of the Box: Because the Dean's services spoke, so to speak, for themselves, 'and as they will ever remain monuments to your glory, we imagined it needless to make any inscription on the Box'.[64] Then, as a further excuse, he adds what he must have known was untrue, and which Swift, in all probability, knew to be untrue, 'and especially as we have no precedents on our books for such'.[65]

Finally, with as much good grace as the unenviable position in which the Corporation had been placed permitted, the Mayor bows to the Dean's demand and concludes – 'But, as so great and deserving a Patriot merits all distinctions that can be made, I have, by the consent and approbation of the Council, directed the Box to you, and hope what is inscribed upon it, although greatly inferior to what your merit is entitled to, will however demonstrate the great regard and respect we have for you, on account of the many singular services your pen and your council have done this poor country'.[66] No such 'consent and approbation of the Council' was ever given, if the Records of the Cork Corporation are to be taken, as they must, as accurate. The conclusion which we suggest as reasonable is that the dissenters refused to compromise, and that the Mayor was left to find a solution without changing the original record, or showing any alteration thereof.[67]

There is no record of any reply from Swift to Mayor Farren, no mention in any further record of the Corporation of the matter – only silence. Swift smarted, however, and never forgave the Corporation. He took the opportunity, in his will, of showing how he felt, by bequeathing 'my Silver Box in which the Freedom of the City of Cork was presented me to Mr. John Grattan, Prebendary of Clonmethan'[68] with the wish 'That the said John do keep the tobacco he usually cheweth, called Pigtail in it'. And that the Corporation of Cork also smarted from the castigation which it received from Swift appears from the unusual step which it took on the 12th April 1738 – 'That no honorary freeman be made for two years, unless some Judge of the Land, or Governor of the Foreign plantations that may be of use to the trade of this City, or Admirals or Commanders of Man of War'.[69] There is an interesting facet of information which appears from an examination of the Council Book of the Corporation of Cork. It will be recalled that following upon Swift's speech at the Tholsel, Dublin, against 'a reduction of the Gold coin', the Cork Corporation passed a resolution supporting Swift's opposition to this course. It went further on September 9th 1737[70] when it instructed its lawyer Coun^r Bennett 'to draw a draft of a Petition to the Parliament in the name of the Corporation showing their grievance by reducing the gold coin, to be laid before this board for approbation'. The member of the Cork Corporation who was detailed to attend on Councillor Bennett with the Corporation's instructions was Augustus Carré,[71] one of the three dissenters to the Swift Freedom resolution. The Petition, when prepared, was subsequently presented to Parliament. In the ordinary course of events one would have expected that Councillor Bennett would have, personally, prepared the draft Petition and presented it to the Cork Corporation. It is, therefore, somewhat surprising to find that he did not do so, that Counsel was retained, and that Counsel was none other than Richard Bettesworth. What is still more surprising is that instead of Bettesworth's fee being paid by Mr. Bennett, it was, personally, discharged by Augustus Carrée and another gentleman named Wood. The Record of the Cork Corporation for 26th Oct.1737[72] speaks as follows: 'That £7.15.0 be paid to Mr. Carrée and Mr. Wood, so much paid by them to Mr. Serj^t. Bettesworth & T. Bennett Esq., for the City Petition about the coin'. This is the only occasion we can trace in the Records of the Corporation on which Bettesworth is recorded as having been retained by, or on its behalf. At worst, therefore, and although subsequent to the date of the Freedom Resolution, we establish an association between one of the dissenters and Richard Bettesworth. That Bettesworth was present in the City, at some time, during the crucial period which followed the Freedom motion is evidenced by Dr. Edward Barry's remark to Orrery – 'I saw here Richard Bettesworth'. And, is there not another strange coincidence in the letter which Lord Orrery writes to Archdeacon Russell at Cork, from Dublin, dated December 21st 1736, and the unusual words used by him in relation to Bettesworth. He speaks of his friends Lord Orkney, Dr. Barry and of the Bishop of Cork, and then, without any warning, says: – 'I hear Dick Bettesworth perambulates your City with a Trumpter before him: Needs he any other Trumpet than that of Fame'. May this not have been an allusion to Swift's 'blast from the proper Trumpet'? And, if it were so, did Bettesworth triumph? The evidence is, admittedly, slight; but there is enough to make us think that Richard Bettesworth may have had something to do with the strange events in the matter of the Freedom of Cork.

Notes

1. For those who require a comprehensive introduction to the matter of Wood's Copper Coins, reference is made to *The Drapier's Letters* by Jonathan Swift, ed, by Herbert Davies (Oxford: Basil Blackwell: 1955) on which this note is based, Swift wrote 'The Drapier Letters' between 1724 and 1725, to encourage the people of Ireland in their opposition to a new copper coinage, authorised by a Patent, which the Crown had granted to William Wood, an English manufacturer, on July 12th 1722, without any reference to the Parliament of Ireland or the Commissioners of the Revenue in Dublin. Wood was empowered over a period of fourteen years to coin more than one hundred thousand pounds worth of copper money, an amount estimated to be at least five times as much as was necessary; and no guarantee had been provided to prevent the smuggling of large quantities of debased money. Swift's series of letters and the policy of an organised boycott of the coinage, which he supported, were mainly responsible for obtaining from Wood a Surrender of his Grant.

2. '...great endeavours are using to get Dr. Swift the Freedom of the City in a Gold box': Letter from Tickell, Lord Carterets' Secretary: Prose Works (Davis) at p. xx *The Drapier's Letters* supra. In 1725 the Corporation of Dublin voted Swift the Freedom of the City; but, four years passed before, on Jan. 16th 1729-30, it was resolved to present it to him in a gold box. On that occasion Lord Allan who had, with the Archbishop of Dublin and the Bishop of Elphin, declined to sign the 'Order for Persecuting' the Drapier (Davis op. cit. xx) took exception to an 'arrogant inscription' for the Freedom box which Dr. Delaney 'with the Dean's approbation' had drafted, and 'wondered how they could complain of Poverty, when they were so lavish as to give a gold box to a man who neither feared God nor honour'd the King, who had wrote a libell on the King Queen and the Government'. See Poems, Vol. 2, p. 494, ed. Harold Williams (Oxford: Clarendon Press: 1958). Swift continuously lampooned Allan in several of his works.

3. Corr. (Williams) Vol. 4, p. 480, Swift and Mrs Whiteway to Rev. Thomas Sheridan. Swift's speech will be found in a pamphlet printed by E. Waters, *Reasons why we should not lower the Coins now current in this Kingdom*: Ibid. p. 480, n. 2.

4. Caulfield: Council Book of the Corporation of Cork, p. 545.

5. Ibid.

6. 18th Nov. 1735: Ibid. pp. 545-546.

7. Letter to Archbishop Wake, Christ Church Library, Oxford. Wake MSS cited by Davis, Prose Works, Vol. 10 p. xxxi, n. 1.

8. Earl of Orrery to Dean Swift. March 15th 1736-37: Corr. (Williams) Vol. 5, p. 9.

9. July 2nd 1736: Corr. (Williams) Vol. 4, p. 510.

10. Christopher Donnellan was son of Chief Baron Nehemiah Donnellan by Martha, daughter of Christopher Usher Esq., of Dublin, which Martha was, after Chief Baron Donnellan's death, wife of Philip Percival, created in 1753 Earl of Egmont. Donnellan was appointed Rector of the Parish of Inniscarra and Mathea, which he held from 1735-1750. He also held, from 1737-1750 the Parish of Kilnaglory, Co. Cork, and from 1745-1750 the Vicarage of Athnowen, Co. Cork. He was a great friend of Swift, and by his Will dated 7th July 1750 he bequeathed a sum of £200 to Swift's Hospital: Clerical and Parochial Records Cork, Cloyne and Ross, by Maziere Brady D.D. (Alexander Thom, Dublin) p. 237.

11. William Meade was the only son of Robert Meade by Frances, daughter of Sir Phillip Courthope of Little Island, Co. Cork. He was born in Cork in 1686. He was appointed Dean of Cork, 1735/6. (Brady, Vol. 1, p. 334).

12. Isaac Goldsmyth was a son of Edward Goldsmyth, Dean of Elphin. He was born at Elphin. He was Vicar of Holy Trinity Cork from 1735 to 1769, and from 1736 to 1769 Dean of Cloyne (Brady, Vol. 2, p. 203).

13. In the disastrous fire which occurred at the Cork Courthouse on 27th March 1891, almost all the ancient City muniments were destroyed... so that the only records pertaining to the Corporation which now exist are such as have been copied by Caulfield and other antiquarians from the original entries. See *English Goldsmiths and Their Marks*, Sir Charles J. Jackson F.S.A. (2nd Edition) (Macmillan) p. 680.

14. Caulfield, p. 560.

15. Ibid, p. 560.

16. Ibid. p. 560.

17. Ibid. p. 560.

18. Ibid. p. 558.

19. Austin's name appears in the Council Book of Cork in an entry of the 27th June 1719 – 'Mr. Sheriff Austin being the fairest bidder for the ground and house called Skiddy's and Bretridges Hospital, ordered, that a Lease be made to Austin for 999 years...' Daniel Engain's name appears first on January 4th 1719 – 'Mr. Dan¹. Engain to be admitted free on the statute during residence. Augustus Carrée was a son of Mr. Gabriel Carrée, who was admitted (on the 16th May 1713) free having married a freeman's daughter. Daniel Engain and Thomas Austin were both sworn as Sheriffs on October 3rd 1728. On the 12th October 1730 Joseph Austin is recorded as being Mayor. Another entry 27th May, 1731 – /Mr. Augustus Carrée, one of the Burgesses, being duly elected, was this day sworn in a member of the Common Council'. The name Austin is a Cromwellian one, being one of the new Cromwellian families introduced into Cork in the latter part of the 17th Century (Windele, p. 16).

20. *The Orrery Papers*, Vol. 1, pp. 155-156.

21. On June 2nd 1723.

22. *In Search of Swift* p. 174, by Denis Johnston.

23. 'Ye Archbishop of Dublin and ye whole Irish posse have (I fear) prevailed with Mr. Marshall (ye lady's executor) not to print the papers etc. as she desired, lest one of their dear joys should be trampled over by the Philistines': Letter dated July 27th 1723 from Dr. Evans, Bishop of Meath to Archbishop Ware of Cantebury. Op. cit. p. 38. Chap 2. n. 23.

24. 'It was a task performed on a frolic among some ladies... and, for my part I

forget what is in it, but believe it to be, only, a cavalier business'. Corr. (Williams) Vol. 3, p. 130.

25. On April 7th Knightley Chetwode wrote Swift, apparently, warning him that copies of *Cadenus and Vanessa* were being shown about in Manuscript. Corr. (Williams) Vol. 3, p. 129 – n. 4.

26. '...they who will not give allowances may choose: and if they intend it maliciously they will be disappointed': Corr. (Williams) Vol. 3, p. 130.

27. 'But what Success Vanessa met,
Is to the World a secret yet:
Whether the Nymph, to please her Swain,
Talks in a high Romantick Strain;
Or whether he at last descends
To like with less Seraphick Ends:
Or, to compound the Business, whether
They temper Love and Books together;
Must never to Mankind be told;
Nor shall the conscious Muse unfold'.
                    (Poems: Vol 2, p. 712).

28. Dublin: Printed in the year 1726. Poems, Vol. 2, p. 683.

29. Letter to Dean Brandreth. Corr. (Williams) Vol. 4, p. 34. (30th June 1732).

30. Corr. (Williams) Vol. 5, p. 23.

31. Swift's services were officially recognised when the Dublin Corporation gave him, as a Freeman of the City, a gold box... The value of this gesture, like that of the box itself, was limited. According to Markaduke Coghill, the Corporation acted only after Swift himself had solicited the honour for three years, and when the gold box was presented, it contained no inscription, although Delaney, at Swift's suggestion, had supplied the Corporation with one... What is lacking in Coghill's account is... that by 1730 Swift had become justifiably embittered by a succession of disappointments... It is understandable that when he received his Gold box – the only tangible reward he ever got for his efforts on behalf of Ireland – he was disappointed that it did not bear an inscription 'showing some reason why the City thought it fit to do him that honour'. Ferguson pp. 185-186.

32. *Advertisement by Dr. Swift, in His Defence against Joshua, Lord Allen*: Prose Works (Davis) Vol. 12, p. 141.

33. Corr. (Williams) Vol. 4, p. 510.

34. Corr. (Williams) Vol. 5, p. 9.

35. See Chapter 1., 'The Scene of Cork' n. 44.

36. Corr. (Williams) Vol. 5, p. 9.

37. Zeus had made Pandora 'as foolish, mischievous, and idle as she was beautiful – the first of a long line of such women. Presently, she opened a box, which Promethus had warned Epimethus (her husband) to keep closed, and in which he had been at pains to imprison all the Spites that might plague mankind; such as Old Age, Labour, Sickness, Insanity, Vice and Passion. Out these flew in a cloud, stung Epimethus and Pandora in every part of their bodys, and then attacked the race of mortals. Delusive Hope, however, whom Promethus had, also, shut in the box, discouraged them by her lies from a general suicide. *The Greek Myths* Vol. I, p. 145 by Robert Graves (Penguin Books, 1955).

38. Swift to Lord Orrery, Corr. (Williams) Vol. 5, p. 21.

39. Ibid. pp. 21-22.

40. Ibid. p. 22.

41. Ibid. p. 22.
42. Ibid.
43. Ibid.
44. Ibid.
45. Ibid, p. 23.
46. Caulfield, p. 552.
47. Corr. (Williams) Vol. 4, p. 510.
48. Swift to the Corporation of Cork. Corr. (Williams) Vol. 5, p. 67.
49. 'That whatever Recorder shall be chosen in the room of the Right Hon. St. John Brodrick Esq., decsd, shall be chosen for one year, commencing 1st May, 1728, and ending the 1st May 1729, unless elected again'. The question being put who should be Recorder, it was carried by a majority; for Eaton Stannard Esq., 11 for Hugh Dickson Esq., 7; for William Chartres Esq., 2: for John Crone Esq., 1; Caulfield, pp. 476/477.
50. Caulfield, p. 477.
51. 'Mr. Sandys told me some days ago, than when he waited upon you for advice, upon some papers that concern the greatest part of my little fortune, you were pleased to tell him, that you should not take a fee if I were to pay it. I owe myself extremely obliged by such an act of generosity and friendship, to which I never had the least pretension, further than the merit of always professing a true esteem for you'. Letter from Swift to Eaton Stannard, 12th December 1733: Corr. (Williams) Vol. 4, pp. 215/216.
52. Letter from Swift to Eaton Stannard, April 11th 1735: Corr. (Williams) Vol. 4, p. 319.
53. Letter from Swift to 'The Right Worshipful The Mayor, Aldermen, Sheriffs and Common-Council of the City of Corke': Deanery House, Dublin, August 15th 1737: Corr. (Williams) Vol. 5, p. 67.
54. 'The Substance of what was said by the Dean of St. Patricks to the Lord Mayor and some of the Aldermen, when his Lordship came to present the said Dean with his Freedom in a Gold Box': Prose Works (Davis) Vol. 12, pp. 145-148.
55. Ibid. p. 148.
56. Corr. (Williams) Vol. 5, p. 67.
57. Ibid.
58. Ibid, pp. 67/68.
59. Ibid. p. 68.
60. The Mayor of Cork to Swift: Corr. (Williams) Vol. 5, p. 68.
61. Caulfield records the following meetings of the Cork Corporation as having taken place between Aug. 5th 1737 (the date of Swift's letter) and Sept. 14th 1737 (the date of the Mayor's reply) – 22nd August 1737, 1st Sept. 1737, 9th Sept. 1737. There is no record of any discussion on the Swift letter. It is safe to assume, however, that there must have been informal discussion for some time, resulting in a compromise whereby the Mayor would write the Dean without any record of the course taken, or the reasons for the award of the Freedom, appearing in the Books of the Corporation.
62. Corr. (Williams) Vol. 5, p. 68.
63. Ibid.
64. Ibid.
65. Apart from the reference to the Duke of Dorset (op. cit.) see n. 46, the following excerpts from Caulfield speak for themselves: 'June 2nd 1733 – That John Croker Esq., Agent in Dublin for this Corporation, be presented with his freedom

in a silver box for the good services he has done the City': p. 524: 'Dec. 16th 1734: That Christopher Swift and Mr. Hugh Winter be made free of this City, on account of their services done to the trade thereof': p. 539: '30th Sept. 1731 – That Thomas Prior Esq., of Dublin in consideration of the great services done to this kingdom be presented with his freedom in a silver box' p. 504: '3rd December 1730 – Unanimously, agreed that Thomas Corker of the City of Dublin, March, for his good services to the City, to be presented with his freedom in a silver Box': p. 498: '22nd April 1728 – His Excellency the Lord Carteret, Lord Lieutenant, having showed his great friendship and regard for this City, especially in relation to the Bay and Woollen Yarn which so much concerns the interests and welfare thereof, it is ordered that his Excellency be presented with his Freedom in a Gold Box of about 20 guineas or £25 value, and that Thomas Clutterbuck Esq., his Excellency's Secretary, being also serviceable to the City, on the same occasion be presented with his freedom in a Silver Box'. p. 477.

66. Corr. (Williams) Vol. 5, p. 68.

67. That the Box was returned to Swift bearing an inscription is confirmed by George Faulkner who has a note – 'In consequence of this letter (Swift's letter to the Corporation) there was an Inscription and the City Arms of Cork, engraved on the Box. And the Reasons in the Parchment Scrip for presenting him with the freedom of that City'. (See Corr. (Williams) Vol. 5, p. 68, n. 1).

68. The Revd. John Grattan and his brother, the Revd. Robert Grattan, were sons of the Revd. Patrick Grattan D.D. and they were both friends of Swift. He frequently visited the Grattan family at their house at Belcamp, County Dublin. Dr. Patrick Grattan's eldest son, Henry Grattan, was grandfather of Henry Grattan the Statesman. John Grattan graduated (T.C.D.) with a B.A. degree in 1698, and he was Rector of Raheny from 1704-1719. He was Prebendary of Clonmethan, 1720-1741, Perpetual Curate of St. Nicholas Within 1731-41 and Prebendary of St. Audeons 1741-54. (Communicated by Miss Geraldine Willis, Librarian, The Representative Body of the Church of Ireland).

69. Caulfield, p. 573.

70. Ibid. p. 567.

71. Ibid.

72. Ibid. p. 569.

73. Barry to Lord Orrery, April 11th, 1736: *The Orrery Papers*, Vol. 1, pp. 155/156.

Index

sition to the Clergy's petition 82; is attacked by Swift and Rev.William Dunkin, 82; effects of attacks on his practice and health 82; fights back 82, 88, 89; first reaction to Swift's attack 83–85; alleged lack of legal ability 85; 'Bettesworth's Exultation' 86; time on his side in fight with Swift 87; moves against Swift through George Faulkner 88; complains to Irish House of Commons 88, believes Swift author of 'Quadrille' 89; forces Swift to retreat 89, in bad health 82; his presence in Cork noted by Dr. Edward Barry 95, 104; his reason for hating Swift 96; reasons for suggesting that Bettesworth behind the objection to Swift's Freedom of Cork 96; is suspected by Swift of complicity in objection to his receiving Freedom of Cork 99; is aware of Lord Allen's objection to Swift 97; fears about Bettesworth expressed by Swift 99; only occasion on which he is retained by Cork Corporation 104; his fee paid by Augustus Carre and Wood 104; his presence in Cork noted by Dr. Edward Barry 95, 104; Lord Orrery's strange reference to Bettesworth and a Trumpter 104

113

First published in the Netherlands
Made and printed by Bosch, Utrecht